BIG BROTHER

ACCESS ALL AREAS

PAUL FLYNN

Books

TRANSWORLD PUBLISHERS
61-63 UXBRIDGE ROAD, LONDON W5 5SA
A DIVISION OF THE RANDOM HOUSE GROUP LTD

RANDOM HOUSE AUSTRALIA (PTY) LTD
20 ALFRED STREET, MILSONS POINT, SYDNEY,
NEW SOUTH WALES 2061, AUSTRALIA

RANDOM HOUSE NEW ZEALAND LTD
18 POLAND ROAD, GLENFIELD, AUCKLAND 10, NEW ZEALAND

RANDOM HOUSE SOUTH AFRICA (PTY) LTD
ISLE OF HOUGHTON, CORNER OF BOUNDARY ROAD AND CARSE O'GOWRIE, HOUGHTON 2198, SOUTH AFRICA

PUBLISHED 2005 BY CHANNEL 4 BOOKS A DIVISION OF TRANSWORLD PUBLISHERS

BIG BROTHER UK 2005 PRODUCED BY ENDEMOL UK PRODUCTIONS FOR CHANNEL 4
ORIGINAL FORMAT BY ENDEMOL NETHERLANDS B.V.
LICENSED BY ENDEMOL NETHERLANDS B.V.
BIG BROTHER IS A TRADEMARK OF ENDEMOL NETHERLANDS B.V. AND IS USED UNDER LICENCE.

TEXT COPYRIGHT © PAUL FLYNN 2005

THE RIGHT OF PAUL FLYNN TO BE IDENTIFIED AS THE AUTHOR OF THIS WORK HAS BEEN ASSERTED IN ACCORDANCE WITH
SECTIONS 77 AND 78 OF THE COPYRIGHT, DESIGNS AND PATENTS ACT 1988.

A CATALOGUE RECORD FOR THIS BOOK IS AVAILABLE FROM THE BRITISH LIBRARY.
ISBN 1 905 026080

BOOK DESIGNED BY M2 GRAPHIC DESIGN WWW.MTWO.CO.UK
ALL SCREENGRABS COURTESY OF CHANNEL 4
ALL FIRST-NIGHT AND EVICTION HOUSEMATE PHOTOGRAPHS © TIM ANDERSON, EXCEPT KEMAL PHOTOGRAPHS PAGES 124,
125 © ANNA BRAITHWAITE. ALL HOUSEMATE PUBLICITY HEAD SHOTS BY AMANDA SEARLE. ALL HOUSE PHOTOGRAPHS BY
JAMES FRY EXCEPT PAGES 20–21, 56–57, 59, 61 BY TIM ANDERSON; AND PAGES 62–63, 99, 101, 113, 115, 129, 131 BY DAVE
KING. PHOTOGRAPH OF SHARON POWERS PAGE 108 © EM FITZGERALD. WHILST EVERY EFFORT HAS BEEN MADE TO CONTACT
COPYRIGHT HOLDERS, WE APOLOGIZE FOR ANY ERRORS OR OMISSIONS.

BACK COVER PHOTOGRAPHS BY AMANDA SEARLE.

PRINTED IN GREAT BRITAIN BY SCOTPRINT, EAST LOTHIAN

1 3 5 7 9 10 8 6 4 2

PAPERS USED BY TRANSWORLD PUBLISHERS ARE NATURAL, RECYCLABLE PRODUCTS MADE FROM WOOD GROWN IN
SUSTAINABLE FORESTS. THE MANUFACTURING PROCESSES CONFORM TO THE ENVIRONMENTAL REGULATIONS OF THE
COUNTRY OF ORIGIN.

ACKNOWLEDGEMENTS

PAUL FLYNN WOULD LIKE TO THANK:
PARTICULAR THANKS MUST GO TO DOUG YOUNG AND SARAH EMSLEY AT TRANSWORLD FOR THEIR
INCREDIBLE PATIENCE, HARD WORK AND VISION ON THE PROJECT, AND TO MARI ROBERTS FOR HER
FANTASTIC COPY-EDITING. THANKS TO MATHEW CLAYTON AND MANDIE HOWARD AT CHANNEL 4 CONSUMER
PRODUCTS FOR THEIR HARD WORK. SHARON POWERS, PHIL EDGAR-JONES AND ALL THEIR BRILLIANT,
CREATIVE PRODUCTION STAFF AT ENDEMOL FOR MAKING BB6 SO UTTERLY ACE AND WITHOUT WHOM THERE
WOULD FRANKLY BE NOTHING TO WRITE ABOUT. ANGELA JAIN, SHED SIMOVE AND ZOE CARTELL AND THE
PRESS OFFICE HAVE PROVIDED INVALUABLE SUPPORT FROM CHANNEL 4. THANKS TO LYNNETTE EVE, DAVID
EDGELL AND DUNCAN YOUEL AT M2 FOR MAKING THE BOOK LOOK AS BRILLIANT AS IT DOES. JULIAN
STOCKTON, PETER BERRY AND EVERYONE ELSE AT THE OUTSIDE ORGANIZATION HAVE BEEN ACE, AS HAVE
STEFANIA ALEKSANDER AND HER LOVELY CARE TEAM, WHO FACILITATED MY MEETINGS WITH THE
HOUSEMATES. FOR ALL THEIR HELP WITH FEATURES: DANNY BELL AND KARL WARNER, TONY GREGORY, DENIS
O'CONNOR, PATRICK WATSON AND PETER DYKE. THANKS ALSO TO JO KNUDSON AND HER WEB TEAM FOR
THEIR WORK ABOVE AND BEYOND THE CALL OF DUTY ON OUR BEHALF. ONE LAST, BIG THANKS TO PAUL LOUIS
WHO HAS BEEN INDISPENSABLE, AS EVER, THROUGHOUT.

CHANNEL 4 BOOKS WOULD LIKE TO THANK:
VANESSA AYIKU, AMY BARTLETT, SUZY BROGARD , RACHEL CARIM, CATHERINE CORNER, CATHERINE
CRAWFORD, RIA CUNNINGHAM, STEVEN EDWARDS, CHARLES FEARN, ROGER FIELD, EMMA FITZSIMONS, VICKI
FORREST, JAMIE FRY PETRINA GOOD, SIAN PIDDINGTON, FRED TOWNSEND.

CONTENTS

INTRODUCTION

BIG BROTHER 6

2005

Three days before the start of Big Brother 6, I was taken on a whistle-stop tour of this year's house. While sitting on the new, improved, huge diary room chair, I had a chance to consider for a moment where we are up to with Big Brother now. It is so much more than a curiosity, a jolly annual bun fight, a glimpse into the otherwise unscreened recesses of human nature or an exciting television game show. It is, frankly, a national institution.

And that was before any of the mayhem had commenced. From the first, tentative footsteps that Derek Laud took into the house to the second Anthony Hutton stepped back over the threshold to a torrent of cheers and fireworks as winner, there has quite literally not been a dull moment in there.

Each Big Brother has its own unique character, and Big Brother 6 was marked by its incredible explosiveness. But amid the general state of delirium, some subtle storytelling was allowed to blossom and some extraordinary characters allowed to tell their own unique tales. These were stories that had not been told on TV before, behaviour that had not been seen and lines that absolutely could never have been scripted by even the most fantastic wordsmiths. Because all Big Brothers are ultimately marked by their own brilliant and sometimes brilliantly toxic humanity.

Behind the veneer of the game show these are the stories that are being told every day and night across the country. Did you see anything on Big Brother 6 that you haven't seen on a

Friday night out in any town centre? Probably not. You might not have seen people dressed up as a chicken or wearing latex nurses' uniforms before. You might not have seen them trying to commandeer a pirate ship or acting as Miss Russia, but the genius of Big Brother has always been in its absolute celebration of ordinary folk in all 360 of their contradictory degrees, its elevation of human nature to a status equal to that of drama. The reason you have never seen these stories before on TV is only because people haven't been clever enough to spot them and turn them into fiction.

So to Big Brother 6. Without it we wouldn't have seen an awful lot this summer. We wouldn't have seen a man falling in love with his friend played out in real time and the two of them resolving this unspoken attraction with a confused but gentlemanly under-standing. We wouldn't have seen the complications a kiss-up in a swimming pool can cause. We wouldn't have seen one man's choice between popularity and money refracted through a 60-second 'red mist' that left him in tears. We wouldn't have seen the clever ways that human beings try to deceive one another for their own personal advantage, or the incredible fallout when those deceptions come back to haunt them. Neither would we have been saying '1 million per cent', 'schoolboy error', 'Alreet!', 'Oh My Days', 'D'you get me?', 'babydoll', 'off the hook' or any of the other house catchphrases that slipped swiftly into popular usage.

Here were the ambitions of the new working classes laid bare, that dream of growing up and becoming a glamour model or selling fitness videos or doing personal appearances as themselves or getting magazine deals or any of the other aspirations that have crept into the modern psyche. Here were the contestants waiting in the wings to see if they could jostle for position in the Celebrity Age. Here was the way that a generation deals with its sexuality.

Some other thoughts. Had you ever thought what it's like to be a male Muslim who enjoys wearing stilettos or an African nurse who looks in the mirror and sees a princess before her? You probably have now. Did you know that 70s dancing still has a following in the north-east of England or that gay black Tories actually exist? Yep, you do now.

Since Big Brother 6, every single argument on the top deck of a bus now finishes with the retort, 'End of!' And just when you thought it couldn't get any more everywhere, Big Brother 6 taught us one of the various uses for an empty white wine bottle. OK, this one we might've known already, but no one would have had the gumption to do it on telly and suffer the outraged reaction to it. What Big Brother 6 understood with timeless accuracy is that nothing is ultimately as shocking as watching ourselves do the things that we do.

Writing the Big Brother book is a bit like having a hit single with somebody else's song. Ultimately, then, it is up to the real authors to take the credit for the amazing stories that are here. To Mary, Lesley, Sam, Roberto, Saskia, Maxwell, Vanessa, Science, Kemal, Orlaith, Derek, Craig, Kinga, Makosi, Eugene and Anthony: well, thanks one and all. Let's hope this does you the justice you all deserve. It was, truly, great knowing you.

▲ Science

▲ Saskia ▼ Lesley ▲ Craig

▼ Vanessa ▲ Makosi

◀ Anthony

Entrance Night

▼erek ▼Roberto

▼Mary ▲Sam

▲Maxwell

◄Kemal

chapter one

WEEK 01

Ultimately, it's difficult not to think of Week One as The Makosi Show. Under the expert guidance of Big Brother himself, the little princess played out her own, one-man psychological drama, her fellow housemates quite oblivious to the scheming going on behind their backs. There were suspicions – on the evening of day 5 Science had muttered the words 'secret mission' in relation to her, only to forget them the next day – but everyone was left largely floundering in the shadows of her brilliance.

WEEK 01:

The Makosi Show

Big Brother is watching you

She introduced duplicity, secrecy and subterfuge into the house within two hours of being there. Which is pretty much precisely what you want from Big Brother from the off. She would ultimately be responsible for the first one of their heads to roll and the first eviction (poor Mary!). At times she looked like she was, if anything, actually a touch too good at the game. In a house full of chattering, bickering, snogging, arguing and slowly bonding characters – almost all of whom could be referred to as 'larger than life' – it was the 24-year-old cardiac nurse from Zimbabwe who ran away with the opening credits. That she did it mostly wearing a candy-striped bikini, wooden bangles, outsized sunglasses and one almighty afro was just a cute little detail in her supremacy. In Week One, Makosi rocked.

But first, some introductions. Meet the housemates. On Friday 27 May, 13 new contestants were introduced to the gigantic human chessboard of the Big Brother house. As if the gods were chiming in accordance with the event, it was the hottest May night on record for 15 years. First minced in Derek, a 40-year-old political analyst and speech-writer. Gay, posh, black, Tory, bald: everything a Big Brother cartoonist could wish for and more.

He waltzed in wearing a natty tailored jacket and denims, before uttering to himself the first words in the house – 'Home at last!' – surely a phrase he had been practising for the entire two weeks in hibernation before arrival. Joined by Lesley, sporting a kinky PVC nurse's uniform that had stuck indelicately up her knickers on the way in, the leery 19-year-old Huddersfield temp took one look at the house and a further look at her housemate before letting out that dreaded Northern calling card: 'Oh. My. F★★king. God.' Already it was clear that

First minced in Derek, a 40-year-old political analyst and speech-writer. Gay, posh, black, Tory, bald: everything a Big Brother cartoonist could wish for and more.

opposites were unlikely to attract. Next Sam, a 23-year-old marketing student, looking like a ringer for Victoria Beckham in *Spiceworld*, only prettier. Lesley didn't like that. What would she have said if she had heard Sam's videotape played out on air before her grand entrance? 'I am the horniest girl in England.'

No doubt someone who would be more instantly in tune with her lusty appetite, Maxwell joined the none-more-curious gang. A maintenance engineer of 24, he instantly betrayed his cockney swagger with his greeting to Samantha: 'You are bang in trouble.' No, Lesley wasn't keen on that either. Derek managed to feign a smile, Sam herself a coquettish giggle. Vanessa, a 19-year-old sales assistant, joined the throng. She complimented both the girls on their choice of attire, Lesley's perhaps more out of shock than anything else. Her own little black dress got the required affirmative response in return.

Anthony danced his way up the catwalk outside the house and managed to incur the first boos from the notoriously undisciplined and hard-to-please Big Brother crowd. There's milking it, sunshine, and then there's body-popping in a *Reservoir Dogs*-type suit and interesting facial hair ensemble. As it turns out, Anthony is part of a 70s dance troupe in his native Durham, as well as being a trainee hairdresser. He is 23. Sam eyed him up within 30 seconds of his arrival and Lesley charged over for her slice of the action. 'Is that a Wonderbra you're wearing?' he asked, noting Lesley's voluminous bosom (she would later confess to having the largest breasts in Huddersfield, 'Apart from me mam's. And me nan's.'). 'Cos it's certainly doing wonders for me.' Cheese!

Roberto's accent instantly became a point of interest as the 32-year-old teacher strode manfully in, sounding like the missing link between Luciano Pavarotti and Ringo Starr. White shirt unbuttoned to the navel, hair slicked back and sly smile as wide as the ocean, he had that definite 70s aftershave ad feel to him: when men were men and brutes wore Brut.

... he was one part prince to ten parts princess. 'Come on, headscarf, don't fail me now, bitch!'

Then Makosi. Her chiffon orange strapless knicker-hugger dress, her heels, her magazine-cover-ready makeup. That glorious 'fro. This was not a woman, as soon was to become apparent, to be messed with. Twenty-year-old Norfolk hairdresser Craig could not help but be a little underwhelming after that sharp dose of film premiere glamour, but his boy-band uniform get-up (white suit jacket, v-neck t, jeans) tried its best.

Despite getting her hood caught up in her chaperone's car and failing to psychically deduce that she needed to actually open the front door, white witch Mary made a mutedly dramatic entrance. 'She's a witch,' bellowed Lesley. 'Are you?' inquired Roberto. 'That's an aspect of me,' the quiet 31-year-old Irishwoman confirmed. 'Do you cast spells then?' joined in Vanessa. 'Sometimes,' said Mary. 'Wicked,' they all agreed. Sadly, they would not get to see one.

The intriguingly named Science mooched through the door in what looked like his granddad's cardy, cornrows, a baseball cap and a t-shirt bearing the immodest legend, I AM AN ICON. His name caused predictable ructions. 'What, Science?' quizzed Maxwell, clearly aggrieved by the ludicrousness of it all. 'What, like Maths, English, Science?' 'Yeah, man,' responded Science, all hip hop like, in what would turn out to be one of his few responses not rising to any bait that week, 'like the full, whole caboodle.' If Lesley had, as her audition tapes had hinted, been a little off with the arrival of pretty girls, Saskia's entrance caused an affront to her dearest assets, those blessed mammaries themselves (the two things it had already become clear were closest to her heart, not just physically). 'F**kin' hell, look at you! Are yours real though? Are they real?' The 23-year-old promotions girl from Surrey assured the blunt-speaking Lesley that they were, indeed, real. At which the Huddersfield lass ran off in contempt to conspire with Samantha – for the last time – about the likelihood of this being the truth. When Sam appeared not to care, Lesley began chewing her fingers in nervous realization that somebody may have bigger breasts than her and THEY MAY EVEN BE REAL. Ah, Big Brother. It's good to have you back.

Lastly, Kemal entered the house. It had to be last, really. Kemal's entrance was probably the best Big Brother entrance in the show's history. In full Muslim red and gold bridal regalia and matching stilettos – a look the whip-thin 19-year-old Turkish student explained as being to symbolize his 'wedding' to Big Brother – he struck a pose outside his chaperone car that almost silenced the braying crowd. Demonically working the runway with a fabulous intergender strut, he was one part prince to ten parts princess. 'Come on, headscarf, don't fail me now, bitch!' he declaimed at his train as he descended the staircase into the house. The housemates, by this point awash with new people, could only stare. His brash resolve soon had them talking again. To call Kemal's entrance both brutal and strident would be to damn it with faint praise. When it became clear later on launch night that his parents knew nothing of his cross-dressing antics or even his sexuality, it was uncovered as almost heroic.

Watching the housemates sizing each other up, casting wicked glances from side to side and realizing that their game plans probably meant nothing now they were faced with the actual competition, it was tempting to do as Derek did and call it an early night, retiring to bed with a cold flannel. But that would have been to miss the main event. Makosi's mission.

There were other things that happened in Week One. There were two parties – firstly when Makosi left the diary room on that fateful first night and rewarded the housemates with a launch bash (canapés and a splash of booze), and secondly to celebrate Mary's 32nd birthday on day 4. In accordance with her gothic bent, everyone dressed as ghouls and danced, some-what incongruously, to Take That. Some false starts were made. At one point Mary and Saskia looked like they might be friends, as Saskia comforted the white witch through her initial wobbles. They hated each other minutes later.

Mary was one of three who cried in the diary room and asked to go. The others were Derek and Science. There were two major arguments. Science fell out with Kemal on night 2 over the largely blameless issue of how to cook a chicken and later on over how 'ghetto' he was. Science made a fuss about the lack of salad cream to go with his fish fingers. Science upset Roberto and they had a huge row on day 3, too. Science mostly fell out with everyone, in fact. Saskia and Mary's argument came from nothing but Mary's instant dislike for the more confident housemate, and it was hard not to empathize at least a little with Saskia.

Now that Big Brother is officially a phenomenon and the housemates are hyper-aware of what works on screen, there are certain

things that are to be expected in the first week, of which rowing is one. Lesley vs Maxwell joined Saskia vs Mary and Science vs everyone as they had a to-do over the Monday mini-task in which everyone had to perform a rap about a fellow housemate. Maxwell committed the heinous crime in his of saying that Sam was pretty and also of drawing attention to Lesley's breasts, something she herself had done nothing but do since arriving.

The other expectation is nudity. Which we also got. Within three minutes of Lesley being let out in the garden she had walloped her mighty breasts out in the plunge pool.

We also expect friendships to strike up that don't look like they'll last the course. Vanessa and Craig slotted into that role, neatly, without doing much else. We expect a lot of brow-furrowing and hair-pulling as housemates realize what they've let themselves in for (hello, Roberto! Hello, Derek – though perhaps without the hair pulling). We don't expect people to bathe in the bin, but we got that anyway with Kemal, who was second in the popularity stakes behind Makosi come the week's end.

What we do expect is a bit of flirting, snogging and intrigue. By night 1 Anthony had put himself in the lothario role in the house – when he wasn't busy following Maxwell around – by

'I don't really know Vanessa, apart from having snogged her.'

dint of a three-way kiss with Lesley and Vanessa. Lesley would later say, hilariously, to Big Brother, 'I don't really know Vanessa, apart from having snogged her.' Maxwell's early predilection for Sam lasted all of approximately three minutes. Perhaps he was a little alarmed by her suggestion that he looked as if he'd be good in bed. 'I can't do anything now, can I?' he confided to Big Brother, rather sweetly in the face of his usual bravado.

So if there are many things by now that we expect, it is the show's producers' jobs to throw in stuff that we don't. Which is precisely where Makosi began to sparkle.

An hour after entrance, Big Brother called for any one of the contestants to enter the diary room. In accordance with the producers' decision to up the housemate quota to 13 this year, they decided to make the 13th housemate unlucky. In many ways the success of the first show (which in many other ways means the success of the series) rested on whoever entered the diary room that night. Luckily it was Makosi. After being told by Big Brother that she was automatically up for eviction next week, the dynamic dear squealed: 'AAAAAAAAARGH! Why didn't you tell me!' She was then told that the only way to save herself from the public vote was to get the highest number of housemate nominations. To make herself, in short, the most unpopular housemate.

Easy. She set to her mission with theatrical aplomb. Watching the other housemates fall for her act was like watching falling skittles. Every one of them succumbed. Watching her bravura performance throughout the week, as she intimidated, argued with and irritated every one of the housemates, it was easy to see why early on Roberto suspected 'she's an actress'.

Insults were thrown around with abandon, suggesting she secretly enjoyed the opportunity to be able to upset everyone. A camp side of both Kemal and Derek seemed to rather enjoy her, though Craig looked forever flummoxed.

The added twist to nominations was something nobody else knew about. So, come Tuesday, they all trooped in to condemn their fellow men. Makosi herself felt confident enough by this stage that she had made enough enemies to assure her safety and, sure enough, she was right. Sam and Roberto made surprise appearances as the other two most unpopular housemates which actually meant that they too would be exempt from eviction.

What we didn't know was who actually would be up for eviction. On a live Wednesday show, Big Brother called Makosi into the diary room to tell her of her triumph. And that she could nominate two housemates to face the public vote. She hesitated before deciding first on Mary ...

Mary, Mary: she had indeed turned out to be quite contrary. After an hour in the house she had decided she wanted to leave. Then she didn't. At first she had been comforted by Saskia, who by Tuesday she had had a stand-up blazing row with. There was a lot of crying with Mary. She blamed PMT, but it was clear from watching her spend more time than anyone either alone, in bed, in tears or all three, that she wasn't happy there. She promised much and delivered little, ultimately. Makosi positioned her nomination as an act of mercy and it was difficult not to see it like that. Particularly given that her second nomination, Craig, was made with the honest implication that she didn't really like him very much. 'He contributes nothing,' she said, scathingly.

After Makosi was released from the diary room, Big Brother told her that she had one minute before the nominations were announced. She immediately darted over to Kemal, by now her best friend in the house, to let him know of her clandestine arrangement. It was pure TV gold. At the studios, a sigh of relief was let out. Mary curiously asked Craig to wash her hair after she was told of their nominations (was this a religious thing?) and Craig looked mortified. That night he promised, from behind a veil of tears, that he would not compromise his dignity for the sake of popularity. This was put somewhat sharply into question the next night when

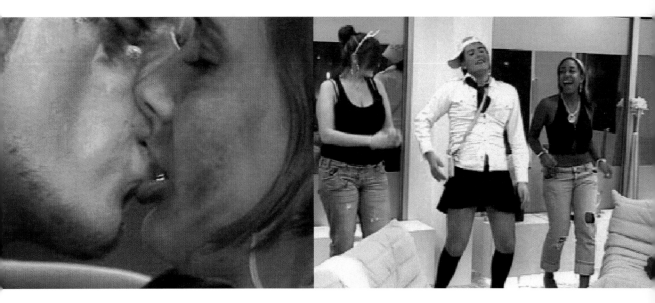

he performed an unprompted a cappella version of Britney Spears' 'Baby One More Time' while dressed as a schoolgirl. The housemates greeted him with a bemused giggle. (Since Darius Danesh's spectacular rendition of the Britney favourite on ITV's *Pop Stars*, the song has long been a reality TV favourite. I wonder whether Craig had that in mind?) Amazingly, it worked.

'He contributes nothing,' she said, scathingly.

So Mary became the first victim of Big Brother's sometimes cruel school of hard knocks. She had been the bookies' favourite to go ever since she was put up for eviction, and she made her exit with far more dignity than her entrance. If she had run into the house cloaked in secrecy, she left in a symbolic crown of roses, all balletic hand gestures and smiles. She had her moment after all. She handled herself with utmost dignity in her eviction interview with the lovely Davina and said she'd been doing it for the money all along.

The house got back to its fractious, argumentative self, almost immediately. Craig looked chuffed to bits.

Profile:

MARY
O'Leary

AGE: **32**
STAR SIGN: Gemini
HOME: London
JOB: Psychic

FIRST IMPRESSIONS: Blimey, she's a Witch! In a cape. With a broom. Seems a little uptight. Little flash of her face. It's very shiny. The cape gets caught, poor love. Heavy eye make-up. Very, very long black hair. A lot of armpit sweat. Khaki dress. Could be very interesting. Rabbit-in-a-headlight eyes. Looks like a very big person trapped in a very small body. Frightened as a dormouse.

Mary was 32 on the first Monday after entering the Big Brother house, an occasion that was marked by a gothic party in her honour. She grew up with her mum and brother in Dublin, Ireland. She says it was a very poor upbringing. She came to London in 2000 and up until going into the Big Brother house was living in a flat in Crystal Palace. She only told two friends she was going into the house. Her own brother, who lives in Tipperary, didn't know she was in there until he saw her on screen. She doesn't have any contact with her dad. Mary does psychic readings for a living but her dream is to be an actress. She says she has 'dipped into' Big Brother in the past and watched it, but not religiously. She does, however, claim to have been abducted by aliens in a previous life and to come from the city of Atlantis. She says she didn't mind Big Brother using footage of her talking about this stuff because 'people can see that I'm a good person. Feck it.' Her favourite thing about the Big Brother house was the gnomes, because they were 'innocent'. Mary O'Leary is the first witch to enter the Big Brother house. She says her hero is Charlie Chaplin.

On Saturday 5 June I meet Mary O'Leary at a photographer's studio in King's Cross where she has just been shot for the cover and will appear in a silky red nightie the following day under the banner headline 'Big Bro Mary: I had sex with an alien'). She seems calm, if a little disappointed to be the first evictee from the Big Brother 6 house. She is chatty and wears the same fingerless black lace gloves she wore to enter the house on launch night.

Why do you think you were the first housemate to be evicted from Big Brother 6?

It took me a while to settle in because my emotions are really close to the surface. When I went in I said I was going to be myself and I guess that didn't give me any protection. I felt quite vulnerable. It took me about six days for my emotions to settle down. And I had bad PMT. Bad PMT and an emotional disturbance is a disaster. Ironically, by yesterday I'd really settled in and wanted to kick ass in there. Unfortunately I was voted out.

Why do you think that was?

I think people thought that I didn't want to stay. There was only 10 per cent between me and Craig though. It was bittersweet for me because I love Craig and I want him to blossom into the diva that he is.

A lot of your criticisms of other people, like Sam, were for not being confident. Was that projection?

Yes, to a degree. I have very low self-confidence. Since coming out of the house, though, I feel a lot happier.

Was this about getting confidence for you?

Subconsciously I think that's true. I've held myself back a lot in my life. I've turned down a lot of opportunities due to a lack of self-confidence and self-belief. I have got so much out of this. I like myself a lot more. I went into that house afraid of the crowd. I came out loving them.

You went in wearing a mask and came out in a crown of roses – it looked like you'd been liberated!

Thank you for saying that. Big Brother was the most amazing experience I could have wished for. I just wish I could have stayed.

Were you a fan of Big Brother before you went in?

Yes, but I've never watched it religiously. I saw the

advert for the audition and I said to my friend that I might go for a laugh. He said I'd be good on it because I'm so quirky. I had a hangover the day of the auditions. I felt like crap but I still went. I got up and said feck it, what else am I doing today? Washing clothes? Tidying my flat? It felt like there was a synchronicity to it all the way through. I felt like it was a thing of destiny, somehow. When I started doing well in the auditions I thought, feck this, I would love to earn that amount of money. That would be my dream come true.

Can you explain witchcraft to a layman?

I believe there's a bit of witch in every woman. Witchcraft is essentially the power of the female form, in tune with nature and the environment.

Wouldn't it have helped you in the house to have used a few more witchy skills?

Like psychic readings for people? Maybe. If I had stayed in I would have done that but I wanted people to know me as Mary first before I got boxed into that. If I was in there now, maybe I'd be doing that. I never really let the wild gypsy in me come out.

Were you aware that you might have been cast on the witch angle?

Feck, no. There are hundreds of witches out there. I don't believe I was cast because I was a witch. I believe I was cast because I'm a multi-layered individual with a lot to offer and I'm sure that the producers were just as upset when I left last night as I was.

Have you watched yourself on TV yet?

No. But I will. And cringe, probably. What was I like?

There's a lot of hair involved.

Well, I have a lot of hair.

Do you regret your big argument with Saskia?

No I don't. The reason I didn't fight my corner more was that I felt her argument with me was very insecure and immature with a lot of low blows. Very schoolyard bully. I don't like her as a person. I think there's a falseness to her.

What are your feelings towards Makosi and the fact that she put you up for eviction?

I don't think she can be trusted. She was quite a close friend of mine in that house. She knew my emotional state. But it was a compliment because she saw me as a threat. She's very intelligent. It's a very intelligent year. Even the less intelligent ones are playing the game.

Who do you think will win?

I think Kemal will win it. It's obvious that he is playing a very, very clever game. He's my tip.

BB Entrance

chapter two

WEEK 02

There are girlfights. There are bitchfights. There is mortal combat between two ladies. And then, somewhere in the stratosphere above them all, there is the drama of Lesley vs Sam. Welcome to Week Two.

The first hints of Lesley's intense dislike of Sam were heard on day 9. Sitting on the orange sofas in the living room, the busty madam let fellow housemates Kemal, Makosi and Craig into a secret: that Sam had invited Anthony to share her bed on their first night in the house and that the rippling Geordie buffster had said

WEEK 02:

Fight fight fight..

no to Sam's brusque advances (does it get any more brusque than 'Fancy a shag?'). Lesley took no small pleasure in retelling the tale of her enemy's rejection. No one looked particularly surprised at Anthony's doing it: who is really going to shoot their bolt on day 1? Decorum, kids, please.

The withering glances between the girls went up a gear on the evening of day 10 as Lesley decided to hide Sam's makeup bag. Bearing in mind that Sam had showered every day since arriving in full make-up, complete with ruby red lipstick, it would be reasonable to assume that going for her No7 was pretty much finding a suitable Achilles heel. But it could have been anything, frankly, such was the antipathy between the girls by this point. They duly descended into a Vicky-Pollard-esque tirade of 'Who you calling a f**king bitch, then?' to unsurprisingly little peacemaking avail. Neither came out of the fight smelling of roses.

By the following afternoon a colder war had been declared, and fearful that nobody was looking out for poor Sam's wellbeing – Derek had snapped at her, too, after an innocent comment about the cooking – Kemal decided to chant for her happiness. If there was one thing Kemal couldn't have been accused of in

Weeks One and Two, it was not knowing what worked on TV. He was in a minority of one, though, when it came to supporting poor stricken Sam, by now very much the loser in the schoolyard catfight with Lesley.

Lesley was showing alarming signs of putting herself in the firing line – nobody really likes a bully, even if they're bullying Sam – a fact that was only heightened when Vanessa scuppered the nominations by talking about how she wanted the 'f**king bitch' removed and would like everyone to join her in nominating Sam.

'Who you calling a f**king bitch, then?'

No matter, everyone had done it anyway! Triumph? Alas not, as Vanessa had broken a fundamental Big Brother rule – now everyone would face the vote on Friday. Gutted.

From the moment this was announced, Lesley started to look like she was skating on some very thin ice indeed, particularly with those heavily wobbling breasts. Her vote-getting, under-the-covers lesbian kiss-up situation with Makosi and Vanessa may have helped matters a little but for the fact that it, too, was later uncovered as a ruse to get at Sam and her default sidekick, Saskia. By day 14 it was clear that if she spent another minute in the house, Sam would be using her makeup bag to find cover-up for two big black eyes. Lesley later said her threats were empty but who could not confess to feeling a chill wind blowing through the house when she warned that she'd be waiting for Sam after they left the house, in the manner of a classic barroom – bra-room? – bust-up.

Things were a little more muted upon Mary's exit, and in true Big Brother style some unlikely characters began to emerge as public favourites. There is little so effective as a task in bringing out the theatrical side of the housemates, and the hospital task, in which the house became an

A&E ward – complete with a matron (Roberto), three nurses (Science, Saskia and Vanessa) and patients (um, the rest of them) – dutifully fulfilled promise by turning them all into No Angels.

After the previous week's Britney farrago, it came as no small shocker to see Craig emerging to the fore. If his cutting humour has yet to be fully developed, it was showing nascent signs of brilliant cruelty. On watching Roberto and Kemal fight for Mary's bed, he turned away distastefully, muttering, 'Can you believe they've already skanked that poor cow's bed?' He declared himself to hate sex and pondered upon Anthony's sexuality – a suspicion Lesley would air later after being chucked out. By this point Anthony had been following Maxwell around so much that he had actually morphed into his shadow.

As if to disprove any such arbitrary and scandalous theories, Makosi had a rummage in Anthony's shorts to check him out for size, under the covers. She later declared him more than satisfactory ('It's this thick,' she said, coiling her thumb and forefinger to a chunky girth, 'though I don't know how long'). Her running commentary as she continued her exploratory search was one of far too few Makosi highlights in Week Two, though Anthony's observation – 'She's playing with me

willy. RIGHT NOW!' – was further evidence of the Geordie's tireless dedication to stating the obvious at all costs. Makosi's strip for Science also proved a moment of titillation, though her boast – 'I got him hard!' – was later disclaimed by the willing victim. 'Actually it's only semied. It's not rock.' Later in the week, Big Brother would give Makosi a repetitive strain injury in her right wrist, tying her raunchy antics to the week's hospital task rather wonderfully.

As younger housemates allied themselves to new groups and seemed to settle into their groove a little more in Week Two, the oldies but goldies had a hard time all round. Derek spent a lot of time complaining about everything, at one point asking Big Brother in the diary room for the direct intervention of the Prime Minister into his plight. Unlikely, but always worth a shot. If Derek kept much of his rage about his fellow housemates to himself or the cameras ('Can you please lower the blinds so I don't have to look at these ghastly, ugly people,' he implored while removing his eye patches, after having been water-bombed by Lesley in his sleep one night), Roberto was less forgiving in his direct-action approach to group problem-solving.

Let's not forget he's a teacher, but Roberto, honestly, was reducing Makosi to tears over the washing-up entirely necessary? Was the stand-

'She's playing with me willy. RIGHT NOW!' – was further evidence of the Geordie's tireless dedication to stating the obvious at all costs.

up row with Kemal in which he accused the youngster of a lack of respect for his parents absolutely on-message? Kemal sailed through that one with dignity intact and called the Italian up to the loft for a private conflab. 'I have lost respect for you,' he said, straight-faced, 'and you will not destroy me emotionally. I am too hard.' Again, it was a gala performance from Kemal. Roberto attacked some of the hospital task with gusto, but mainly he ran round complaining about food and the lack thereof. Food was becoming his thing.

Surprisingly, Craig jumped into the older fuddy-duddy camp and began complaining about everyone's antics. Particularly Anthony and Maxwell's decision to eat Oxo cubes and wee themselves 'for a giggle'. 'That made me sick,' he said, cowering for full effect, 'for 24-year-olds to stand there and piss themselves.' Unfortunately, Craig was pregnant with Big Brother's baby at the time and wearing a blue sundress, somewhat messing with the gravitas of his disgust. His giving birth to a gnome, accompanied by birthing partner Lesley, was surely the highlight of the hospital task, which, predictably, the house failed with flying colours, ensuring Week Three's shopping budget would be a mind-boggling £77.

The big Science/Maxwell water fight on day 9, which resulted in Science being both reprimanded by Big Brother and having to sleep in the living room after throwing a bin at the lairy Cockney, was one of the few bust-ups of Week One proportions. It came, it went and the boys grudgingly made up the next day. They both found allies as a result of it. Science in the curious form of Derek, no less, who seemed to compare the young rapper to Mahatma Gandhi and Martin Luther King before saying he was 'the best young role model in the house', just a touch too soon (he was throwing the bin two hours later). And Maxwell in Saskia.

Here was the great offsetting tale of the week. If Roberto was scrapping with everyone, Lesley sealing her fate against Sam, Derek showing intense signs of aggravation and Craig emerging with a delightfully vile little aside for every occasion, it was left up to M&S to spread some love. Bless. These were the seedlings of a proper little romance. First off the blocks to confess their feelings was Saskia. 'He is just one lovely, lovely guy,' she told Big Brother after the bin-throwing escapade.

Though she says she doesn't fancy him, the next afternoon she hops straight into that classic girl flirtation technique of saying she looks ugly. 'Hats just don't suit me,' she said to Maxwell, pouting in the mirror at top strength. 'Yeah they do,' he replied, bang on cue. When she next asked Sam, 'Can you fix my bra strap?' you could see the blood rising in Maxwell, already a strong favourite and emerging with a surprisingly robust moral centre. Their flirtation continued hotting up, gathering pace through-out the week.

As a reward for winning the counting mini-task in which everyone had to dress up and count as high as they could (she reached 261!) while enduring the hurling insults of Big Brother, Saskia was rewarded with the ability to be Big Brother. Told that she could call any one housemate into the diary room and feed Big Brother three questions of her choosing to ask them, she plumped straight for our Max. Watching him on a secret TV screen in the bedroom toilet, Saskia saw him declare his feelings for her, quite voluntarily: 'She's off the

hook to look at and a gorgeous girl. She's probably the person I have the most of a laugh with in here, as it goes.' Aw!

'She didn't start off at the top of my list,' he continued, referring to his initial soft spot for Sam, 'but she's head and shoulders above the rest of them now.'

Later Craig put himself in the frame again by sidling up to Maxwell with a hosepipe. 'Do you fancy Saskia?' he quizzed, ever quick off the starting block. 'Do bears shit in the woods?' Maxwell indiscreetly confessed. They had a brief conversation about her, Maxwell making the startling revelation that he went for a girl's personality as well as looks. 'There's nothing gay about that,' assured his new buddy.

And they were the week's winners, really. Craig lost a sparring partner as Lesley was unsurprisingly booted out come Friday, wearing a PVC policewoman's get-up to complement her arriving nurse's outfit. 'Sergeant Sexy' was emblazoned across her right breast. It was a fitting epitaph. She hadn't been happy at all for the last couple of days and ended up venting her wrath on Sam. Lesley's target hung on by the skin of her lipstick to fight another day.

Profile: LESLEY Sanderson

AGE: 19
STAR SIGN: Sagittarius
HOME: Huddersfield
JOB: Temp

FIRST IMPRESSIONS: A Carry On nurse in PVC. Spectacular. Truly spectacular. Knickers seem to be stuck up her bum. No matter. Looks very nervous. Enormous chest. Not good with those stairs. Keep your eyes on her: she could be amazing.

Lesley lives in Skemthorpe, Huddersfield with her mum and dad and three brothers, 15-year-old Paul, 13-year-old Jamie and 10-year-old Kieran. She says that her mum is her closest friend and that when she learned she was going into the Big Brother house her mum was the only person she told. Lesley finished her studies in Performing Arts at Huddersfield Technical College last year, where she specialized in dance. She was working as a temp – 'mostly admin' – immediately before entering the Big Brother house. Her big love is clubbing and her favourite record to dance to is 'Hungry Eyes' by Eye Opener ('loving that one'). Her favourite club is Visage&Ethos in Huddersfield where drinks are three for one. She took one of the Big Brother production team down there when they came to check out her home environment, and partly attributes getting into the house to this. She says the woman couldn't believe how many people she knew in there, and she confesses that this may have something to do with the three-for-one offer. Lesley says that she has a loud mouth and that her hero is Christina Aguilera: 'I think she's gorgeous and fab and that she's absolutely beautiful and if she walked into a room all eyes would be on her.'

Lesley arrives on my doorstep less than 24 hours after her eviction. Now, when a housemate professes to be chuffed to be out of the house, you tend to think they're lying. With Lesley it seems like nothing but the truth. She is so much softer – and slighter – in the flesh that she is almost unrecognizable. Then that great Yorkshire voice booms out and there's no mistaking her. She laughs a lot more than she did in the house, is a lot more likeable (you'd merrily go down the disco with her) and has a surprising line in teenage wisdom. She looks delighted to be back on terra firma. I think it all got a bit much for her. Bless.

How are you feeling?
Brilliant. I'm so happy to be out and to see my family. I've never been away from home before. Well, I was away for a week once but I phoned my mum about ten times a day.

You're a self-confessed mummy's girl – how did you possibly expect to cope without her?
I don't know! It sounds stupid but I just thought it would be a laugh in there. But it wasn't, obviously. We argued all the time. I couldn't cope without my mum or my dad or my straighteners or my friends or clubbing or shopping.

What was the worst argument?
The one between me and Sam. I wouldn't normally lose my temper and be that much of a bitch, but being away from home and everything …

You basically projected all your unhappiness onto her?
Basically. I felt ground down and I wouldn't normally threaten anybody. But I couldn't stick her either. She annoyed me from the first day. She loved it if I had a problem with Maxwell or Anthony. She'd just let out that stupid little laugh. She's insecure, I don't think she's got any proper friends. I do feel sorry for her. I told the other housemates that she wasn't right on the second night. They'll find out. Actually, I think she fancied me.

Have you watched yourself on TV yet?
Yeah and I'm really disappointed. I look like a proper minger on telly. I didn't have my GHDs in there so my hair's not as straight as it should be.

When did it strike you that it wasn't for you?
As soon as I started missing my hair straighteners. It's so sad but that really was the biggest thing for me.

Where did you get your nurse's and police outfits from?
Off the Internet. It was my mum's idea. You only walk into the Big Brother house once and you only walk out once. I wanted to make a statement.

Did the boos upset you when you came out?
I'm not sure. I was thoroughly booed though. Was I upset? [thinks] Yeah, a bit.

You seemed a bit obsessed with your knockers. Do you think about them that much in real life?
Oh yeah. Course I do. That's why I thought they'd given me that neck brace in the hospital task, so I couldn't see them and go on about them any more. They are me best asset.

Do you look at other girls' boobs before you look at their faces?
Yeah, probably. Just to make sure they're not bigger than mine.

Were you a little bit jealous of Saskia's?
Here's my thing about Saskia. You know Lucy Pinder, the glamour model? She won't show her nipples. I think Saskia's the same. She knows that Lucy Pinder's more lusted after because she keeps them hidden and she gets more money because of that. I know Saskia already does promotional work, so that's obviously in a bikini. I think she's being pretty clever with those boobs. I cannot believe Sam's had a boob job, though. They're so small! If you're gonna have a boob job, make it worth your while!

Were you worried about anything coming out in the papers while you were in there?
Yeah, I were shitting myself about it cos my ex-boyfriend's got rude pictures and videos of me. I asked him for the sim card back but he wouldn't give it to me because he said it was a gift from me to him, which is fair enough. I had to trust him.

What's your thing about mushrooms?
They just give me the creeps. They're ugly, disgusting and foul. I started working as a part-time waitress and my phobia came from there.

Did you enjoy anything about being in the house?
Yeah, I enjoyed the water fight. I enjoyed Mary's party. I thought she was a bit strange at first because I'd never met anyone like that before, but I liked her in the end.

Who do you think is going to win Big Brother 6?
Craig, definitely. I'm not just saying that because he's my friend. He's beautiful and brilliant and I love him to bits.

INSIDE THE DIRECTORS' GALLERY

First, a little geography. The directors' gallery for the live Friday-night evictions is just to the right of the Little Brother set in the huge cavern of the Big Brother studios. It is a small, prefabricated building with really useless air conditioning. You wouldn't think it was the nerve centre of Friday's tense live TV broadcast, but it is.

A bank of TV screens at the front of the gallery is faced by nine seats in rows of three. The screens display the different camera angles and from these the director decides what you, the viewer, see on the show. There are lots of buttons and knobs and flashing lights on the desks in front of the seats. I don't know the purpose of any of them but I think it's best not to rest my bottle of water on one. There are several people going furiously through sheets of notes on clipboards; some of them have headsets on. Being in the nerve centre of a live TV show that's being watched by millions of viewers is weird on every level. I hold my breath and observe.

Barring the presenters and housemates, every bigwig involved in Big Brother 6 is in the gallery for Friday's show. In the middle of the front row, Series Director Tony Gregory shouts instructions, loudly but calmly, into his headset. Behind him, Executive Producer Sharon Powers and Creative Director Phil Edgar-Jones chip in their opinions. Channel 4 Commissioning Editor Angela Jain sits on the back row, quietly.

I sidle into the gallery just before the 9.30 show. This is Lesley's eviction night, and there is no small excitement. Nobody on Big Brother is allowed to show prejudice to any housemate, but it is fair to say that Lesley has been popular with the production staff. She has made the effort for her eviction, of course, donning that tremendous PVC-edged policewoman's get-up, much to everyone's delight.

The first half of the live show runs smoothly. There is a cut to a videotape (VT) of her last half hour in the house, which, what with this being Lesley and everything, offers up a predictable dose of 'oh f**king hells' and the like. She looks nervous but steely on many of the cameras and I flatter myself that I can see exactly why Tony selects the shots he does, while marvelling at the precision and dexterity of his timing. When Davina goes up to collect the strapping Huddersfield lass from the house, the team are confident enough to find new angles for the shots and frame presenter, housemate and braying audience against the wall of the house with the Big Brother black and blue eye superimposed. 'We're going to go a bit arty,' instructs Tony, and instantly it's done.

The second half of the show is Davina's interview, but first the staff must compile the last shot of Lesley's exit for the VT to play of her time in the house at the end. Tony gets an operative to replay her climb up the stairs in comedy quick-time, then slowed down, then quick again, fearful that you can see her knickers on one of the shots. He finds the shot.

'Lose that,' he instructs.

'Do we need to?' asks Sharon, completely at one with the fact that this is a girl who has chosen to leave the house in a skimpy PVC policewoman's uniform.

'I think it's her,' agrees Phil.

The shot stays.

Back on air, Davina's interview is predictably brilliant. Her touch with the housemates is that uncanny television mix of questioning and sympathetic. To say she's got a common touch is to damn her with faint praise. She genuinely appears to love people. Though there is a producer in the gallery feeding her lines, I hear her speak only three times and I never hear Davina repeat verbatim what she's given – it always has a bit of Davina's marvellousness added.

Whenever Lesley talks of a fellow housemate, Tony directs a camera to find them on the sofas in the house and project them onto the screen behind her and Davina. Predictably, it is Sam who features mostly, demonstrating facial expressions you just couldn't invent. Though booed, Lesley is calm, funny and perfect TV. As the closing credits are quickly counted in, an imaginary glass is raised to her in the gallery. Everyone liked her, a lot, and you can't help feeling there is a little sadness at her going.

For a live-TV virgin, the gallery is a heart-pounding experience. For the Big Brother team, it is an amazingly calm affair. I'm impressed.

chapter three

WEEK 03

WEEK 03:

Allegiances

Big Brother is
watching you

Ah! The irony. So we began the week after the hospital task with two housemates' ankles in plaster. 'What is the likelihood of that?' pointed out Vanessa helpfully, after she had drunkenly bounced between beds only to take a cracking tumble in a rare combination of personal momentum and joy. So the young shop assistant joined Saskia, who had twisted her ankle, in the Accident and Emergency of real life, fresh from their fictional rendition of the same set-up. And the naysayers still insist that Big Brother cannot do life

imitating art imitating life? Absolute rot! And there's your proof.

Lesley's departure left the house feeling a little less Asbo than usual. As usual, out of sight was out of mind, and after a couple of drinks even her (ample) bosom buddy Craig seemed to have forgotten her existence. For a whole morning there was a lull, a little moment of quiet. As Lesley swanned off to join the other former Big Brother contestants in the celebrity ether, Craig and Vanessa were left with the uphill struggle of finding new allegiances to keep themselves in the game. Some little subsets had already emerged. With whom would they align? With the oldies, somewhat overkindly referred to on the Big Brother website as Team Sensible, Roberto and Derek? Or with the little triumvirate of Saskia, Maxwell and Anthony, fast becoming the alpha corner after enjoying their cheers from the Big Brother crowd when Davina read their names aloud in the eviction process? (Nothing does more for a housemate's confidence and cheer in the strange micro-world of the Big Brother house than supposed public affection. It is what they are in there for, after all.)

Or how about the more tantalizing subset of Makosi and Kemal, looking quietly strong in the dressed-up corner? Neither Craig nor Vanessa was ever likely to plump for Science, who by now was looking unafraid to stand alone, or Sam, who, alas, was looking like she had no choice but to stand alone. As Vanessa gravitated towards Kemal and Makosi, Craig lingered around Saskia, Anthony and Maxwell, the bizarre love triangle. Nothing becomes a housemate more than a couple of willing ears.

Week Three was what hardened Big Brother watchers refer to as a classic. It was clear that

'I'll have a better time in that box than I would in the house,' countered Roberto.

the production team were working at full imaginative, and slightly demented, strength when 11 boxes were placed strategically around the house, each emblazoned with photographs of a housemate and with warning signs – 'Hazard', 'Handle With Care', 'Highly Flammable' and the like – daubed on their sides. This was supposed to be a mini-task. The task team behind the scenes had said they imagined the housemates would manage somewhere in the region of two to three hours in their boxes, at the very most, and Big Brother offered the reward of a slap-up dinner and access to a luxury fridge for the housemate who could stick life under the box for the most time. Little did they account for the reactions of those oldies-but-goldies, Roberto and Derek. When confronted with the idea of a brief spell in solitary confinement, their little faces lit up. It took years off them, frankly.

'I love my box already!' whooped Derek.

'I'll have a better time in that box than I would in the house,' countered Roberto, whose issue with the food or lack thereof had now come to absolute, arm-flapping crisis point.

'Yes,' agreed Derek, 'what on earth is there to miss?'

Anthony revealed a previously unseen competitive side. (Don't take him on at table football, kids.) Some took a more practical approach to the mini-task. 'I'm going to have a wank,' Maxwell declared. Ever resourceful, that boy. Of the girls, Makosi warmed most to the idea. There was a suspicion, later confirmed, that Sam would be a little too fidgety for this sitting-still stuff, though she, too, joined in the idea of it as an excuse for a session of self-love and perfected a highly polished fake orgasm while within, swiftly telling Big Brother that it wasn't 'real or nothing' afterwards. She also said she was doing this to put Anthony off, though her actions later in the week around the sex-starved north-eastener would suggest otherwise. Vanessa was equally predictable in her box and stayed mostly silent.

Science was first out of his box (what a creature of habit), with the belting and memorable refrain: 'Science cannot be contained!'. He instantly slipped into mischief mode and, after being rewarded with a plate of bacon sandwiches, took the dripping and began slipping it through the holes in Kemal's box. He was next out. Sam followed not long after.

And then a strange thing happened. Saskia and Maxwell's boxes began copulating with one another.

'Where's your hole?' asked Maxwell, in a somewhat ungentlemanly though impressively forthright manner. 'You should be able to wiggle it through here,' answered his paramour.

After their fast building affection in Week Two, Saskia and Maxwell, to the trained Big Brotherly eye, started looking on way more shaky ground in Week Three. It was fast becoming apparent that what Saskia saw in Maxwell was a sort of safety zone around a popular housemate, confirmed by the cheers he had received on the night of Lesley's eviction. What he had seen in her, however, was a girlfriend. He would later admit this to Craig in one of their bouts of man-to-man dating advice, as he confessed to punching above his weight, knowing Saskia to be a catch the real world would possibly not have afforded him. All interesting stuff, particularly as it began to isolate Saskia and Maxwell from the rest of the group, who were at their most sceptical because of that very cheering. Psychological intrigue. What the game was invented for.

In the end, the idea of the boxes mini-task lasting three hours was a wild fantasy on the part of the task team backstage. For health and safety reasons they had to let the three winners – Anthony, Roberto and Derek – out after 26 hours and 16 minutes in the box. But every minute of it had been startling television. A brief pause to comfort poor Makosi who had given up the ghost only an hour earlier, missing out on the luxurious fodder of the prize. 'Big Brother,' she declared as he announced the winners, 'you are such a wanker.'

The three chaps emerged triumphant from their boxes to a round of applause from the housemates. Were they finally beginning to bond as a group? Watching Sam with still only a bikini as a best friend, it was difficult to think so. But time was beginning to march on and some softness was becoming apparent elsewhere. Strangely, Vanessa emerged as a calming influence on the rest of the crowd.

The main task of the week was overshadowed by the sheer simplicity and quiet genius of the boxes. But nevertheless, as the house was transformed into a pirate ship, there were plenty of opportunities for the voiceover artist on the Big Brother television show to make lots of jokes about seamen (what with it being such a comic-sounding word and everything). The group's pirate song became a thing of mild lunacy, and Craig's face was a picture as he blah-blahed along to it in the rain. But the housemates were true to their utterly useless weekly task form and had managed to spunk it – good work, seamen! – with a record 27 fails by day 19. On the same day Science threw a cup of water aggressively into Kemal's face over a petty washing-up incident, incurring his first formal warning from Big Brother, yet beginning his own real psychological journey in the house. He had proved hugely unpopular as captain of the pirates, and appeared to regress into his own world to ponder this. It took some pondering.

Later in the week he would provide the emotional peak of the game thus far when he

'Where's your hole?' asked Maxwell, in a somewhat ungentlemanly though impressively forthright manner.'You should be able to wiggle it through here,' answered his paramour.

apologized to Kemal in the love loft by baring his real name, Kieron Harvey, in what was a moving display of genuine and touching remorse. Kemal took the apology like a man. It was difficult not to recollect his refusal of Roberto's apology after their Week Two argument and to see Science emerge the bigger man than the older Italian. Hadn't Kemal and Science been the ones at each other's throats when they had first met, too? One fazed by the stiletto-wearing theatricality, the other by the self-styled ghetto eccentricity. It was a beautiful thing to watch them make up in a quiet but conclusive manner. Sometimes this Big Brother thing can make you cry, if you think about it long and hard enough.

But this was a mere trifle compared to the other grand upset of piratical Week Three. It was while acting as a lookout, with one casual eye to the telescope, that Derek began a superbitchy tirade against Saskia and Maxwell that would later rebound on the other housemates involved in this tête-à-tête.

'She is a silent assassin, Saskia,' he began from the vantage point of the crow's nest. 'She's orchestrating it all.'

'She is,' agreed Roberto.

And the conversation went on like this:

Roberto: 'She is orchestrating everything.'

Derek: 'The big way of clipping her wings is by putting her up for nomination. They're harbouring under this belief of their popularity because they got cheered and so on and so forth.'

Craig: 'Have you not noticed the change in people since that night?'

Derek: 'They think they're invincible.'

Craig: 'They think they're superior in every way.'

Big Brother would never stand for this behaviour, of course, and action was swiftly taken. That afternoon the housemates were asked to nominate for the third time. Though they are always invited into the diary room in alphabetical order, the line skipped from

Anthony to Kemal, missing out Craig and Derek. Later Roberto was excused his turn, too. Craig steadily turned a brighter shade of pink the longer his exclusion lasted. Derek and Roberto tried to appear unflustered but something was clearly amiss.

After everyone had nominated, Big Brother pulled a blinder and dropped down a plasma screen TV and played the bitching back to the gathered throng on the sofas. A black cloud descended. Craig's instant 'yeah but no but yeah but' mortification was almost comic.

Maxwell flipped his lid, declaring the older housemates 'f**king wankers'. Saskia sat coolly throughout it all, confirming her alpha status. It was a stoic, magisterial performance. The best we had seen her yet. 'I'm cool as a cucumber,' she said, with one of those girlish smiles that says underneath I'm raging, but you're not having any of it, 'because I'm fine. I just feel that people can discuss what they want. You don't have to like me. Say what you like about me.' And then the killer: 'Dog eat dog. Let's see who wins. End of!'

Superb! Derek, Roberto and unlucky, unliked Sam were to face the public vote.

On day 20, ironically the same day in series 5 of Big Brother that is now infamously dubbed 'fight night', Big Brother lightened the atmosphere

with some bouts of speed-dating. An orgy of sorts ensued.

Already Makosi had taken the understandable step of turning Anthony into her sex toy, straddling him on the bed and fiddling with the contents of his pants when the fancy took her. Anthony attempted to cover his nerves with bravado through all this, but the princess was making mincemeat of him. Was she attempting to curry favour from the audience after seeing the Saskia/Maxwell effect? Or was this sizzling frottage a more innocent endeavour?

They went for the snog on their date in a moment of steaminess rarely seen before in the game. Not to be outdone, Saskia and Maxwell kissed, too, though their individual reactions (Him: 'That was off the hook!' Her: 'That was hilarious!') said all you needed to know about the lady's increasingly sisterly approach to him. There was a strange, almost unnerving moment between Roberto, in his usual exciting underwear, and Kemal, as they played out a one-act drama up there in the love loft that looked like it might emerge into something more sexual. And Derek wore women's clothes and used Mrs Thatcher's oft-repeated catchphrase, 'The Lady's not for turning!'

Ultimately, the love loft was not only a brilliant diversion from the dramas elsewhere in the house, it was the night that Sam effectively signed her death warrant with Big Brother. Having initiated a fully fledged, saucy and not altogether unpleasant kiss-up with Makosi, she attempted a lap dance on Anthony. It had all the sexual allure of a wet weekend in Scarborough and Sam confirmed the public's perhaps premature conclusion that she was a little desperate, after all.

Next night, she was thrown to the lions. Davina interviewed her in a bikini, making television, Big Brother and world history. I think the word is 'priceless'.

Profile:
SAM
Heuston

AGE: 23
STAR SIGN: Aquarius
HOME: Surrey
JOB: Marketing Student

FIRST IMPRESSIONS: Pretty. Very pretty. Good walk but could be faking the confidence. Not sure about the funny bob hairdo with straggly bits but she's definitely the house totty. She'll be mowing the lawn naked by the end of the week.

Sam is 23 and has just finished a degree from Oxford Brookes University in Marketing, Management and Publishing. She much prefers men's magazines to women's and doesn't think it's fair that women can't buy mags with naked men in them as easily as men can with women. Prior to Big Brother she lived at home with her parents and brother Chad, 21, in Cheam, Surrey. She is very close to her family, but says she gets a lot of bother from girls. She didn't like school because of this. She considers herself only to be bisexual in the sense that she likes kissing girls ('Not genitals, no') and says she has kissed some of her friends but admits to having played up to it a bit to get into the Big Brother house. Sam has had one long-term relationship that she'd rather not talk about. If she could have any celebrity boyfriend she would choose Duncan from Blue. Her heroine is Christina Aguilera, though she looks astounded when told that this is Lesley's heroine, too ('she never told me that!') and decides on Abi Titmuss instead. 'I think she's funny and rich and doesn't care how she made the money. She's a great sex columnist and she knows a lot about it but there's much more to her than sex.' Sam considers herself to be a feminist. 'Definitely. I think that men and women should be equal.'

I meet Sam on the Monday after her eviction. The day before she has been on the front cover of the *News of the World* under the headline: 'BB Sam: I want to bed Davina (and all my housemates)'. She is all limbs, fidgets a lot, is disarmingly pretty and is wearing very little. She doesn't exude a great deal of confidence, and finds it hard to make eye contact, but otherwise she is an absolute revelation. The giggle is all down to nerves and once she calms down she can be quietly fascinating and very sweet. She's got quite an odd take on life, but it's definitely a take. I liked her so much more in the flesh than in the house.

After three weeks of Big Brother I still feel like I know very little about you, other than that you like sex. Why is that?
Because nobody in there wanted to know me. You can't force people to be interested in you. It doesn't work. In the last week I think there was a conscious decision to blank me. There really is nothing worse. It was like being at school. Saskia in particular reminded me of all those awful hard girls. The cool ones never liked me.

Why did you want to be on Big Brother, Sam?
Honestly? I've always wanted to be famous. I had lost interest in my degree and I thought it was a good way of getting seen. People say that not a lot of housemates become famous, but I thought I would do. My expectations were very low but they were there. And I think I've proved that I have got something since I've been out. [Sam has signed a lucrative deal with *Nuts* magazine.]

Will you be upset if this is the end of your fame?
No, it's quite scary. I'd quite like to go back to normal after this. My two best friends, or supposed best friends, sold stories about me to the papers.

What do you think the producers saw in you?
The fact that I was quite sexual was one thing, definitely. But the fact that I was very honest and upfront in auditions was another. I danced in front of the queue in hotpants at the audition. Everyone seemed to like me.

You are a very good-looking girl. Did that go against you in the house?
With the girls, yeah. And with the guys actually, after a bit. I think Saskia, Anthony and Maxwell wanted me out.

Was it anything like you expected it to be?
I'd prepared myself really well. For the two weeks we were out of action before we went in I'd – and this is going to sound really weird – I'd practised what it was going to be like being watched 24 hours a day. I'd practised breathing exercises and ways of chilling out.

Was it a conscious decision to use your sexuality to win the game?
It was a tactic, yeah. But it is just me at the same time. I am a sexual person. I was hoping that people would be open-minded, I guess. I really thought they would be. I can't tell about these things. What do you think?

I think you used your sexuality but weren't confident enough to be able to look at ease with using it. I think people wanted to see something else as well.
So it seemed a bit fake? I'd never thought of it like that but it's probably true.

Asking Anthony to bed was the moment Lesley decided you were weird. Did you dislike her?
Yes, I did. She's another one of those girls that don't like other girls. Once she called me a desperate tart when I got into bed with Anthony. I mean, it's the 21st century. We're in the Big Brother house. Let's have sex! I thought people liked me after Lesley was voted out. I thought they'd done it to stick up for me because she'd been so nasty.

They did. For Week Two you were fine, but I think the lap dance killed it for you.
I think I probably knew that it would come across as misguided but I didn't sit down and think about it. I just did it. I thought, I'm on telly, let's show off a bit. And worry about it afterwards. I had faith in women that they'd enjoy that side of me. And they didn't.

Who did you first like in the house?
Maxwell. He made it seem like it'd be bearable because he was the one person who was nice to me in there. I thought, I can do this now, but he turned really quickly. Obviously I'm not too keen on him now. He changed his spots in five minutes.

Is anyone in there not playing a game?
Science, I think, is genuinely just strong. I admire him for that. It's easier to be objective once you get out.

Who do you think is going to win Big Brother 6?
Makosi. She is so clever that I felt like I was with an actress for the entire three weeks I was with her. I've never met anyone that clever or with that intuition. She seemed to know things about me before I did.

Why do you like sex so much, Sam?
I don't even, any more. That's the funny thing.

THE HOUSE

The clever man behind the look of the Big Brother 6 house is Patrick Watson. Patrick had his first meeting about how the house should look in early February, just after Celebrity Big Brother had finished. It was his first time designing the whole house, though he had done task design for Big Brother 5 and worked on Celebrity. His initial brief was to make the house as aspirational as possible while still being tricky to live in and claustrophobic. 'It has to look good,' he explains now, in his office up at Elstree, 'but feel hard to live in. These things are fairly difficult to marry.'

He took much of his inspiration for the house from Californian architecture. 'Minimalism is good because it promotes a lack of comfort and privacy. It's very open plan and feels almost like an establishment building.' He decided very quickly to make glass a theme throughout the house. 'A lot of the directors have commented on that this year. That they can get shots of people talking behind each other's backs but still get both of the people in frame. It makes their job a bit easier. Kemal walking into the living room from the bedroom in the thong was a great shot where you could see everyone's reaction in the bedroom while Science and Anthony were horrified in the living room.'

After the first meeting about the house design, Patrick was working on it right up until the housemates entered. The day before opening night a lorry driver was despatched to France on an overnight pick-up to collect the sofas for the living room. 'It can be a bit tense,' he says, 'but you don't come to work on Big Brother if you don't like a bit of that.' The other soft furnishings were gathered over time after the team had chosen a colour palette that, he says, reflects a current vogue. 'For want of a better term, I suppose you'd call it iPod retro. Though the *Daily Mail* called the colour scheme Austin Powers, which I didn't like.' The colours are all bold enough to allow you to recognize instantly where a housemate is at any given point. If it's yellow, you know they're in the kitchen.

Some things will inevitably be remembered from the Big Brother 6 house. I mention to Patrick that I saw the green dog in an interiors shop in Islington, north London, the day before we met. 'Sharon [Powers] picked that up. It works really well on camera.' The diary room chair was hand-made from a design Patrick drew up, inspired by a classic 60s egg chair. 'It had to be womb-like and

comfortable, to draw people into letting stuff out, and it had to be big enough for two or three people to sit in, which Anthony and Craig have used brilliantly.'

The job of the house designer is not just to make the place look fabulous, it's also to allow for practicalities. 'Basically,' says Patrick, 'the idea with the house is for it to function as a TV studio set and obstacle course while still minimizing the physical disruption to the housemates. In previous years they've had to be cooped up in the bedroom while a task has been set up. This can disrupt developing stories, which is what the house is ultimately all about. But there are two distinct areas this year, so when you're setting up tasks or interfering with the house there is still a lot of room for the housemates to roam around and bitch in. It doesn't have a huge impact on their day-to-day lives.'

Of the features in the house this year, Patrick is particularly pleased with the 'fish tank' effect: the soundproof glass wall between the seating area and the bedroom. The white carpets have been less successful as they have been dirtied by all manner of substances. But as Patrick says, 'It's amazing what you can cover up on camera. It looks filthy in the house, but to the audience it's not too bad.'

Everyone else is delighted with Patrick's design. He's just been asked to come back and design the seventh Big Brother house. 'I can't wait,' he says.

chapter four

WEEK 04

WEEK 04:

Room 101

There are weeks of Big Brother when certain housemates shine, when they start to look like stars in their own right. These are the weeks when you look at these normal people – who meant nothing to you a couple of months ago, who were just getting on and not being extraordinary at all – and then you look at the incredible viewing figures and think, hmmm, someone is learning, accidentally, to be brilliant TV. To be great at the game. It is a magical process.

There are other weeks on Big Brother when you look at certain groups of people, little factions, small friendship groups, budding relationships. Then groups become stars. They can be as graceful as figure-skating champions or as clumsy as a rugby first-11, but acting the way they are makes the whole social experiment of Big Brother slot neatly into place.

Lastly, there are the weeks when a sort of calm has settled after a raging storm, where the housemates are falling into patterns of behaviour, allotting themselves niches, becoming familiar enough to us as viewers and voyeurs for none of them to have to be the star of the show, when we are comfortable enough with them being in our thoughts, in our living rooms and on our TV sets, with seeing more of them than our friends, our families and our partners.

It is at this moment that the game itself becomes the star of the show. This was the pivot on which Week Four turned. It wasn't about who was doing what any more. Big Brother became his own star. He just guided his masterful hand over the ten remaining housemates and led them down cul-de-sacs of behaviour that threw their own motives back at themselves. It is weeks like this when I genuinely believe that the show is a work of genius.

The starter was fittingly, but misleadingly, daft. On day 23, the housemates were given a task to incubate eggs while dressed as chickens. Sometimes that is enough. Watching Saskia – by now a kind of dictatorial, alpha ice maiden guiding her little gang of boys: Maxwell, Anthony and Craig – slip into a canary-yellow chicken outfit was to see cool killed in one stroke. As this subset of housemates made it increasingly clear that they were 'the popular ones' and thus wanted as little as possible to do with the rest of the riff-raff, so Makosi's

Big Brother became his own star ... It is weeks like this when I genuinely believe that the show is a work of genius.

affections for her sex toy, Anthony, began to dwindle. 'I go out with people who find me smashing,' she confided, all sisterly-like, to Vanessa, while wearing her chicken outfit. 'I like people who adore me. Me being a girl, me having a brain and him not having one automatically gives me an advantage over him. Good-looking dickhead.' Makosi went on to make a good crack about her being an 'Egg Kosi' but dropped her charge and became the only housemate to fail the task. On announcement of the task being over, Maxwell and Anthony headbutted their eggs with Maxwell actually drawing blood. Boys, boys.

It was day 24, however, when the game really began to gather pace, when the housemates were put to the test to see how duplicitous they could be. The house was turned into a workhouse and housemates were asked to don a uniform, cap and badge and to number themselves. Automatically launching for prime position, Vanessa declared, 'I wanna be number 1!', but was soon ruing her move.

Worker number 1 was asked by Big Brother to clock in for a shift in the fittingly titled Room 101 down the corridor. Here Vanessa was asked to sort maggots according to colour into separate jars. Vanessa was distinctly unamused.

Unamused, in fact, didn't cover it. Sick to the stomach was more like it. She tried the door twice, but neither time made it over the threshold. Eventually, she ran to the bedroom toilet, disrobing, screaming and distraught.

In the end it was Maxwell who gallantly stepped into the breach, taking worker number 1's position. And here's the crunch. For while he was to sort maggots, Big Brother would give secret luxuries to the rest of the housemates. The weekly task was not, therefore, to be part of a workhouse at all, but to kid worker number 1 that they had been doing the same as him while they lapped up a bit of pampering in the garden. It was a brilliant moment to throw this task at the housemates. And Maxwell was the perfect housemate to do it. As Derek pointed out: 'I shan't feel guilty about fulfilling this task for 2 reasons. 1, the joke is against Maxwell, who richly deserves it. And 2, we're actually doing this for the good of everybody, including Maxwell, to get a luxury shopping budget.'

By now, the older wing of the house, Roberto and Derek, had reached the end of their tethers over the lack of shopping. Rarely could Roberto begin a sentence without it referring to the shopping budget, to food or to his role as chef by self-appointment in the house. During Week Four shopping became *the* big issue for the housemates, hardly helped by Maxwell's

mischievous inclusion of an extra eight cans of cider from the previous week's list at the expense of both a chicken and mayonnaise, much to the chagrin of his fellow diners. (Was Maxwell's mischief by now turning irritating? Did he in fact need to perform the workhouse task alone both to redeem himself in the eyes of the housemates and to save himself from the week's public eviction? It was difficult to think otherwise.)

So Maxwell began sorting maggots as the rest enjoyed the blistering sunshine, with a bouncy castle and sweeties on the lawn. Never one to turn shyly away from a sweet product, Vanessa looked repentant for all of two minutes. Maxwell's buddies Saskia and Anthony looked concerned for a matter of seconds only. It was time for some fun in the house. On day 25, while Maxwell screwed oily nuts onto bolts in Room 101, they would enjoy champagne, strawberries and beauty treatments in the garden. On day 26, while Maxwell was dispensed to his dungeon to shell prawns, the others enjoyed high tea, with a giant chessboard, badminton and five bottles of fine wine.

The visual juxtaposition, hardly hindered by the blazing June sunshine in the garden during the hottest week of the year so far, of the rest of the house living it up while Maxwell settled into

On day 25, while Maxwell screwed oily nuts onto bolts in Room 101, they would enjoy champagne, strawberries and beauty treatments in the garden.

some hard and boring labour, would normally have been enough, but the workhouse task also produced its own incidental by-products. Maxwell clearly enjoyed the idea of putting on a show even while doing the most mundane of tasks. Singing and joking, talking to 'himself', he was acutely aware of being on view.

If Maxwell's performance had been a little unnecessarily theatrical, everyone else's had been supremely talented and a simple joy to watch. At last, after the disaster of the A&E and Pirate weekly tasks, Big Brother had alighted on something that the group were collectively excellent at: deceit. On the three days they had to pretend to Maxwell that they too had been doing this unappealing screwing and shelling, they all turned in superb acts. It was almost as if double standards were second nature to some of them. Why, Makosi even managed to pull off a performance, under some strict tutelage from Derek, while drunk. This was beautiful to watch, for it was just an outward manifestation of what they had been doing all along, pretending to the other housemates that they were all on side, while secretly stabbing them in the back and working them over. Which is, when all is said and done, the nature of the game.

Perhaps it was their confidence in the task – which, hoop-la almighty!, they actually passed – or perhaps it was them approaching the one

month mark, but something brought out the philosophical side of the team as they progressed through Week Four. Roberto confided in Derek that 'perhaps we're too old for this game', a statement that would come back to haunt him when first the two older members of the party were put up for public vote by their housemates' nominations and later he marginally won the right to walk the public gangplank on Friday night's eviction. Though it was a tight vote, it seemed like the right one. Roberto had been getting steadily more short-fused with his younger peers, and it was fascinating to think how Derek, the more erudite of the two, would be without his accidental old mucker.

Other bubbling resentments – some surprising, some less so – surfaced. On day 26 Kemal began to question Makosi to Big Brother in the diary room. This had been one of the more enduring friendships in the house, one that made sense visually as well as intellectually, one of the few you could imagine escaping beyond the confines of the house and into the real world. But the stiletto-wearing Muslim diva confessed in a moment of rare uncertainty: 'Sometimes I just feel that it's Makosi, Makosi, Makosi, Makosi. I honestly, myself, cannot deal with not being the most fabulous one! I feel that if I have to stay here much longer the

Whitney/Mariah situation might have to emerge.' His fabulosity had been usurped. The reference to the warring divas was a cute detail, but Kemal was definitely beginning to show vulnerability. Where he retreated into his shell as their friendship came into question, Makosi did as she had done before (with Sam), and adopted a weak girl as a thin piece of armour. Vanessa became her confidante.

Derek's exasperation with Science came to a bungled head when he confessed in the diary room: 'I have met in Science the first black man that would make me want to become a member of the BNP.' Saskia's relationship with Maxwell was beginning to look highly shaky, she veering towards the sisterly affection of a playmate, he clearly enamoured with the headway he'd made on a girl who was, looks-wise at least, way out of his league. Their ever-present chaperone and gooseberry, Anthony, now had his own play-mate in Craig, whom he wrestled delightfully in the diary room.

Though she wielded a certain hard-faced power in her own clan, elsewhere in the house the hatred towards Saskia was beginning to silently boil over. Her aggressive castigation of Vanessa over Maxwell's cider farrago – 'You're a scavenger, darling!' – was hard and ill-judged enough to ensure that she had no female

'I have met in Science the first black man that would make me want to become a member of the BNP.'

allies left by the week's end. Not that it appeared to bother her.

Yet it was Roberto who took the viewers' weekly whip-lashing. The man who had neatly commented on day 26 that 'life is a continuous test', failed his public popularity examination and walked out to face his people in a flowery Primark shirt. There were some cheers amid the boos. Derek began to look like the cat with nine lives. And in the rest of the house something was afoot, as would soon become clear …

Profile:
ROBERTO
Conte

AGE: 32
STAR SIGN: Gemini
HOME: Liverpool
JOB: Teacher

FIRST IMPRESSIONS: How long till someone coins the phrase 'Italian stallion'? I give it five minutes. Big, handsome guy, wearing sparkly shirt open to the navel and hair slicked back. Bit older, could be trouble with the ladies. Looks like he should have a box of Milk Tray in his hand.

Roberto came to England in 1997 from Scauri in Italy. He has a brother, Filippo, and a sister, Maria. He thinks he was always 'the troublemaker and hothead' in the family. He told them that he was going into the house and they are all very proud of him. He loves England, though he feels that we should incorporate kids and old people more into the family, 'not push them to one side'. He has utmost respect for his grandmother, who had Parkinson's disease. He has been a windsurfer and a lifeguard. His last job before Big Brother was working as a PE and RE teacher in Huyton, Liverpool. 'I don't see myself as super intelligent, but I do think that people should have the same chances. It was my choice to work in difficult schools, because they need you the most.' He's grateful for the teachers at his own school. 'I wasn't a model student but I learnt about discipline from them.' He thinks he sometimes comes across as a bit arrogant. 'I can look arrogant because I'm confident. I'm not a saint and I've made my mistakes but I can look myself in the eye and know that I am a good bloke. I don't think I'm bigheaded.' Roberto doesn't have heroes but there are people he would like to meet, including members of Depeche Mode. 'This will show my age, but every time I have been through something in my life, there comes along a Depeche Mode song which talks to me directly about it.'

What a scene! Two days after Roberto's eviction I walk into his hotel and there is a scrum around him. He is an absolute pro with everyone, a proper people-pleaser. Jokers buy him drinks, women swoon over him, kids come up and sit on his knee. He's a formidable physical presence: tall, broad and handsome. He's more intimidating than he thinks he is. His command of English is incredible and he has a clear sense of right and wrong. Like more housemates than ever before this year, Roberto was in it to win it. He looks disappointed to be out of the house, but all the attention is compensating a little.

How does it feel being out?
I would have liked to stay a few more weeks. I think, along with only a couple of other people in there, I was the only one with some morals, some values.

What was your strategy for the house?
To keep busy and to put my ego away. To stop myself going mad. On many occasions I acted like a servant to those people – which I don't mind – and all I asked in return was a little bit of appreciation.

What did you imagine it would be like?
I thought there would be a bigger variety in terms of age and character. I was hoping to find more interesting, wacky, crazy people. In the eviction process I always went to nominate the most boring person in the house. I tried not to be personal and instead think what would make it work and what would keep it entertaining.

You were thinking about the TV show?
Absolutely. The funny thing is that people thought they were very subtle and smart and that they weren't showing they had a plan, but of course they were. I didn't get any stimulation from anybody in there. At one point I thought: at Christmas I need to buy these people a lobotomy.

Who was particularly game-playing in there?
The worst player was definitely Saskia. I'm competitive but I like a fair fight. I definitely didn't want to be aggressive. I don't feel I was. But I don't like people taking the mick. I don't have hard feelings because mostly they were young. When I was 19 I thought that I knew it all, too.

Why did you throw a plate of pasta on Maxwell's head?
To teach him a lesson about being greedy. If you look at everybody in there you can see the greedy ones because they haven't lost weight. I think he's actually put it on.

What about your weird coming on to Kemal in the love loft? What was that all about?
It was about saying you want to play camp, I can play camper.

Were you a fan of the show before you went on it?
I used to follow it in bits and bobs but not religiously. That's probably why I'm here now. If I'd done my revision better, I probably would still be in there.

What do you think the producers saw in you?
I have no idea. I'd love to know. We need to ask them this question.

Was some of the appeal of going into the house to be on TV?
Of course. Everybody likes a bit of attention and there is nothing wrong with that. But it was a combination of things. This is going to sound strange, but I wanted to go somewhere where I could forget about things. I wanted to be in a place where I didn't have to worry about bills and credit cards and my van breaking down. I wanted a bit of an escape.

What's your biggest regret about the house?
That I didn't get to tell my stories. I have so much to tell but there was no interaction between people. This is quite a popular strain of thinking this year, everyone who comes out seems to be saying 'if only the people were different I would've been all right'.

Don't you have to take some responsibility for this yourself?
Of course you do. I tried, but there is a very strong awareness of the cameras.

Is there anyone among the younger characters in there who interests you?
Kemal and Craig are interesting. Science could be but he frustrated me. He is a good bloke, underneath, but he demands things. People do want everything on a silver plate now.

Was your favourite bit of the whole experience the boxes task?
Yeah, because I didn't really feel challenged in there, mentally or physically.

Do you regret going in at all?
No, I don't. I think I'm the happiest man on the planet and I am enjoying passing on some of that positivity to people who need it. I feel love coming out of each one of my pores.

Where on earth did you get your amazing selection of underpants from, Roberto?
H&M. I buy all my clothes very cheap. My entry shirt was £5 from Burtons.

Who is going to win Big Brother 6?
Derek, if there is any justice. He is the only reasonable character left.

Secret Garden

chapter five

WEEK 05

WEEK 05:

Secret Garden

The week began with a bit of a backstage line-up shifting as three new housemates made their first Big Brother appearances. For some reason they were bedecked in an ornate arrangement of fig leaves and swimwear. This became one of them, the Irish temptress Orlaith (she went out with Calum Best, you know!). It gave ample opportunity for another to scratch about in her nether regions – 'Bloody hell, me minge!' declaimed Kinga as her opening shot (one she would struggle to better). And for the third, a radio engineer called Eugene, with bleached tips and a goofy, nerdish gait, well, it would reduce

Eugene to tears within a day of being a secret housemate, for fear of being laughed at. Crumbs.

The three secret housemates were dispensed into a secret garden, which wasn't a garden at all, of course, but a little room with a ring hob and a double and single bed arrangement, covered in plastic greenery and with a talking stuffed stag on the wall.

The three new secret housemates provided brilliant entertainment. Kinga's initial foray into Big Brother land may have lasted only three days, but this short stay was packed with what can only be referred to as 'Kinga-isms', an unsubtle soup of profanity and youthful exuberance, with particular attention to the detail of everyone's reproductive organs.

When discharged into the real house to gather as many supplies as they thought they would need without being found out, she emerged triumphant from the fridge with a cucumber and brandished it in a frankly appalled Eugene's face. 'You can use this to stick up me fanny,' she helpfully explained. Alas, we would have to wait until Kinga reappeared spectacularly in Week

Ten before we could find out what further pearls of wisdom she would dispense as a fully integrated member of the house.

On day 30, a red buzzer was erected next to the diary room in the house proper, with a double-headed message of intrigue signposted on it. DON'T PRESS THIS BUTTON read the larger legend. PRESS HERE counter-teased a message underneath. It wasn't long before Makosi had taken it upon herself to wallop the little bugger down, setting off an alarm and a demand that she go into the diary room. Again,

DON'T PRESS THIS BUTTON ... PRESS HERE counter-teased a message underneath.

she was headed for a secret mission, this time to feed, clothe, water and bathe the secret housemates in the secret garden and to keep them unknown from the rest of the house. After Big Brother 5's secret bedsit, we already knew that a little room of which the housemates knew nothing could act as the perfect conduit for a major drama, for a seismic ruction in the equilibrium of the Big Brother house. But the secret bedsit would provide the perfect counterpoint for Makosi's scheming mind and the biggest war of the whole series so far.

Much as Maxwell and Saskia might try to make their relationship the centre of the week's dramas, it was impossible not to see another relationship – more fractious and intriguing, more Krystle and Alexis, more stilettos at dawn – to be the crux of the house during Week Five. It was OK Corral for the team divas. Saskia fought a bright and ballsy battle, and her boys proved to be an utterly useless back-up battalion. Makosi, who had chosen her enemy with precision, played her like a fiddle.

Other relationships were building, deflating and emerging in strange configurations all over the house. For Team Saskia, the week was played

Diary Room Eye

out largely against the orange sofas of the living room, where Craig had by now affiliated himself with Maxkia and their ever-present sidekick, Anthony. The four didn't make a particularly appealing sight as they revelled in their own slobbery. 'I haven't lifted a finger since I've been in here,' boasted Saskia. The biggest mistake of Team Saskia in Week Five was relying on former glories. Maxwell's icy self-satisfied grin was beginning to grate. The Big Brother audience likes nothing less than watching housemates resting on their self-perceived laurels. Craig, meanwhile, had started to wear 'fickle' as his primary characteristic: this was at least his fourth friendship group in the house, though he seemed happiest yet with it. He was moved to tears on several occasions by Saskia's prowess as team leader. He cowered in her wake. He looked a bit sycophantic, really.

If there was an interesting gay male/straight female tangent emerging in Saskia's boudoir, the one at the heart of Team Makosi was starting to crumble. Kemal's motives with Makosi were coming under question, most prominently from Vanessa. 'I think he just wants to be you. It's like he's always trying to compete with you. I think he likes what you are about – your look – more than he likes Makosi. If there was no afro and no jewellery and no glamorous clothes, I don't think that he would be your

> 'I think he just wants to be you. It's like he's always trying to compete with you. I think he likes what you are about – your look – more than he likes Makosi.'

friend.' Vanessa had been getting a hard time outside the house from a public bored with her televisually dull behaviour, but sometimes she could be spot on. Makosi nodded in sage agreement with her lady-in-waiting. Kemal himself, as if on cue, had a breakdown in the bedroom. He was not the first to question Makosi's authenticity in the house, but he was the first for whom it genuinely seemed to matter.

The factions reached their peak, and a clear divide emerged. 'I call it us and them,' said Saskia, surrounded by her pups in the living room. 'It's a blatant divide,' added Anthony. To Derek, Science commented, 'All this divide is spoiling the fun,' before adding, somewhat rumly, 'It's not like I like conflict or anything.' Science, know thyself!

Underneath it all, a bleary racial split could be divined, hardly helped by the audition tapes of the more outspoken members of Team Saskia, in which both Saskia and her new admirer Craig had shared some colourful views on immigrants. It was beginning to become uncomfortable viewing from the other side of the screen. In this light, the arrival of new housemates couldn't have been more timely. There are many Big Brother detractors who see the show as nothing more than silly season for

desperate wannabes. It's in weeks like this when you want to force these people to sit down and watch the show and observe its sometimes accidental sociological revelations.

Makosi completed her mission with astonishing prowess, proving once again that no one could deceive as stylishly as she could. On day 31 she even managed a great escape, slithering Kinga, Orlaith and Eugene out of the secret garden and through the house for a shower as the other housemates slept. Even more astonishingly, as the other two cheerfully showered nude, it was Kinga who kept her thong on, protecting at least two inches of her modesty.

And it was also on day 31 that everything reached a heady climax over a stray ten cans of cider. Makosi leapt to the diary room in the evening, knowing that booze was on offer. She took the cider, beloved of Maxwell and the rest of her rival faction, and disappeared into the secret garden to drink it with her new buddies. She reappeared an hour and 40 minutes later, tipsy, and lit the touchpaper of the built-up tension.

Maxwell had been getting more and more riled by her antics. 'She's a f**king idiot and she winds me up. Nominations tomorrow. Can't wait. I hope she f**king drinks them all and dies of f**king alcohol poisoning. It's winding me up that she wants to wind us up.' But when Makosi emerged it was Maxwell's Lady Macbeth who stepped up to the challenge.

'You don't think I drank it?' Makosi baited Maxwell, 'then smell my breath.'

And in struts Saskia. 'I'll smell it.' Which she did. 'It smells of dogshit.'

'You are a f**king bitch and your breath does hum.'

Ouch. And then she was off, sounding her own death knell. 'Do you know what, Makosi? You came in here a bitch, you were cool, you turned into a bitch. You're selfish. You call yourself bullied, you cried. You are a big attention-seeking drama queen bitch. You are not a victim! You're the most powerful person in the house.'

With which, one suspected, we were getting to the real issues here.

'You know how to play everyone. Including yourself. And you do play yourself. You are f**king wrong, Makosi. You've got a chip on your shoulder that people like you do. You're rude. You think you're Jordan? You're mad. Are you buzzing? You're not f**king Jordan. Jordan is a businesswoman and a clever woman and you are not. You are a fake, a selfish bitch who will go nowhere in life. You are a f**king bitch and your breath does hum. You're even wearing a f**king wig on your head. You are a fake girl.'

Call me perverse, but I rather liked Saskia for this. It was the eve of nominations and she showed she had some balls. She confronted the other Queen Bee in the house. She had a show-down, while Maxwell – her supposed knight in shining armour – just stood by and watched. Only Craig from her band of merry admirers tried to spring to her defence, to be rebuffed by Makosi with a scathing and rather brilliant, 'I don't want to hear from you, Team Britney. Not you!'

In the event, Saskia and Maxwell went up against the public, and their response was to find ways of fondling one another as often and openly as possible. As Saskia observed in the garden, 'We're as f**ked as f**ked can be. And nobody ever gets remembered who goes out at this point.' She took her knickers off before diving into bed with Maxwell and he bared his bottom to the world. There were some unfortunate sound effects from Saskia's bangles as she serviced him with her hand. It all looked revoltingly token, though both of them say it wasn't. It was Kemal who aired the public feeling most articulately when he asked them to stop slobbering over one another in the bed next to him. 'I'm sure you've got your magazine deal now,' he said. It earned him a glass of water in the face from an acutely aggressive Maxwell and Maxwell himself his first formal warning. Poetically, it also invited the line of the series so far. 'At least someone got wet tonight and it wasn't Saskia.'

The end of Makosi's secret mission was to pick two of the garden housemates and integrate them into the house. She opted for Orlaith and Eugene. Saskia eyed the Irish beauty with suspicion from the outset as Orlaith waltzed into the house wearing Saskia's towelling tracksuit. Orlaith had everyone fondling her breasts by her second day in the house. She

got to play Juliet in the utterly hilarious Romeo and Juliet ballet task. She pouted a lot and turned out to have a charisma of sorts, behind the make-up. She talked about Calum Best a lot. And she didn't just irk Sask. Craig was also put out by her appearance, as she had obviously taken a shine to his by now beloved Anthony. Orlaith had the affront to make the Geordie a cup of tea, inviting Craig's wrath. As he declared, jokingly, but a little worryingly: 'Nobody else makes him tea. I am the bitch. I am the skivvy. I am the submissive. I am the slave.'

Saskia was probably right to be a bit worried. Two girls fighting for supremacy in the house is good value. Three is a crowd. And then on Friday Saskia was evicted with a towering majority of 71 per cent. I couldn't help feeling that she was a little hard done by. She didn't bother with mass goodbyes, but left Maxwell with the words, 'You're gonna win. I hope you win.'

Derek simply winked at his unbroken team, all clearly loving every second of this from behind a wall of steely silence. 'Justice does always come,' he ruminated, his silent assassin now a memory.

Profile: SASKIA
Howard-Clarke

AGE: 23
STAR SIGN: Aries
HOME: London
JOB: Promotions Girl

FIRST IMPRESSIONS: Definite page 3 look going on here. One for the lad mags. Busty beyond measure. Little dress but likely to be perturbed by Makosi's, which was a bit less high street. Pretty, top heavy, nice hair. Girls starting to look good this year ...

Saskia is 23 years old and works in promotions. This involves a lot of being pretty for a living. She likes her work but wants to step it up a gear, a large part of the reason she went for Big Brother. Saskia lives in Surbiton, south London with her mum, dad and little brother Joshua, 15. They're all really proud of her time in the house. 'They were over the moon. My mum had a tear in her eye when I got booed, but I understand at the end of the day it is pantomime. I'm not daft.' Saskia was born with a hole in her heart that had to be operated on when she was six. At 11 her consultant found a narrowed artery and she had to be operated on again. She has had one grand love in her life, which broke up a couple of years ago. Since coming out of the house she has seen her pre-Big Brother 'boyfriend', but only for 10 minutes. She apologized to him about her very public affection for Maxwell while in the house, but doesn't regret it. 'I'd told him I was going away anyway and not to have any expectations.' Saskia auditioned for the show in London and said she played up her laddy side. 'You know the Melanie Sykes Boddingtons advert? That's the kind of idea I was going for. Nice-looking girl and then she burps at the end of it.' Saskia surprises me when I ask her who her hero is. 'It's Professor Oku, the guy who did my heart surgery. How can someone save your life and not be your hero?'

I meet Saskia just after she's done a set of underwear shots for *Nuts* magazine. She talks openly of being a fan of Big Brother, but she sees it as a stepping stone to bigger things and seems very much in control of her destiny. She's the closest so far in the flesh to what you've seen on screen: straight talking, slightly intimidating, no-nonsense, ambitious, very considered. She's like Martine McCutcheon's harder, prettier, younger sister. She's a stunning-looking girl. She is also ready-cooked for fame and there's no doubt she is one of the housemates you will see more of once this year's show has finished.

How does it feel being out?
It's weird, basically. It's been really hectic and exciting. I've had a busy schedule since I've been out.

Do you think you behaved differently in the house last week because you knew your time was coming to an end? I got closer to Maxwell because I knew my time was up and I wanted him to know it. But I stuck to my guns.

In the big argument you had with Makosi, Maxwell really hung back. He didn't look terribly supportive.
I don't need anyone watching my back. When Derek called me 'the secret assassin' Maxwell was bang in there. He was the first in. I like loyalty and he is very loyal.

How does the Makosi argument make you feel now? It is essentially why you are here.
Yeah, I understand that. But I think she was bang out of order. She was mischievous and deliberately caused trouble. She was playing the game.

Do you think that she was better at the game than you?
I don't think she was better than me. I want to be known as genuine and the real me. My family are proud of me. She can do whatever she pleases and good luck to her, but are her parents proud? She was a pain in the arse.

When the big split happened in the house, were you aware that your time was running out?
Yeah, definitely. But I thought as viewers you'd either like us or them. I was quite shocked at the boos.

I think you got those partly because of how confident you and Maxwell were on Lesley's eviction night.
I was pleased by the cheers that night. Anyone would be. But I did say very clearly to Maxwell after that that you've got to keep those cheers. I wasn't complacent about them.

What did you want to get out of the show?
I trained as an actress but my look was always too 'glamour'. I thought if I did Big Brother I'd get some exposure. I'm not naive and I don't expect anything out of it, but if it doesn't work out then I've earned some money, had a great experience and … let's see what happens.

Lesley thought that you'd decided to cover your breasts up in the house because you know they become more valuable then, like the glamour model Lucy Pinder.
I want men to look at me and think I'm mysterious and sexy and to want me. Once they've seen it, they get bored of you. I want them to undress me with their eyes. Yeah, I know Lucy Pinder doesn't show her nipples and I don't think I need to show them to appear sexy. The way I see this is as a business, and if I can earn money out of this, then great.

You know that people don't believe your relationship with Maxwell was real because you are so far out of his league in terms of looks.
This is the issue, yeah. But none of my boyfriends have been oil paintings and I love a character. I want someone who is good boyfriend and then husband material. I want someone you can stay home with and go out with, someone you can make love with and you can shag. He's a good laugh. I genuinely go for character.

After a couple of days away from him, is it still intense?
It was like a year's relationship in there in a couple of weeks. He is a young lad. If he wants to go off then so be it. I'm not stupid.

Was the great divide a racial split, even subconsciously?
No. This gets so badly on my nerves. If you don't get on with someone it has nothing to do with colour, simple as …

Did you think that going in the house would make you ask questions about yourself?
I do think maybe I'm not as nice as I thought I was. But it's an extreme situation. Normally if you have a row with someone you don't have to see them. In there, it's 24/7.

Do you care what people think about you for getting up to some sexy stuff in the house?
I cared about what my parents would think, but people make their own conclusions, don't they?

The Sunday papers said you had sex in there.
Do you know what? Whatever. Even if I did, I'm in my 20s, I'm a grown woman, so what.

Was there a bit of a maniac in you that you had to try and keep down in there?
Yeah, with a lot of deep breaths. I knew I'd flip if I was pushed.

PETER DYKE

'NOBODY CAN HAVE A CODE TO WIN THE SHOW. IT'S LIKE WATCHING LAB RATS ... LAWLESS, RECKLESS, UNPREDICTABLE'

MR REALITY TV

By PAUL FLYNN

PETER Dyke has been writing about Big Brother for the *Daily Star* since series 1. Such is his professional interest in (and honest-to-goodness love of) the form that he is dubbed 'Mr Reality TV' by his paper.

'Big Brother is a godsend for the tabloids because generally news-wise there's not much happening in the summer. Parliament has broken up and news tends to die so you're looking for new stuff to keep your paper pepped up. Big Brother is the king of reality shows. It was in the middle of series 2 that the papers exploded with it, with the start of Paul and Helen's relationship. When we got hold of pictures of them going off into a love den, the first splashes on 'TV sex shocker' started to appear. That hadn't been seen before. Now the housemates are incredibly canny about what they're getting into, but the producers are always one step ahead. Nobody can have a code to win the show. It's like watching lab rats. There's a lawless, reckless, unpredictable quality that is v difficult to find with other shows. people are volatile and everyb loves a good argument. The vis stuff is gold dust to us, too, and producers are aware of that. T know how to generate press and work very well with them. I thou Lesley and Kemal did a brilliant on launch night, dressing up like t did. She got all the front pages putting on that sexy nurse's outfit really is that simple. Anthony pla it all wrong. With his body,

ORLAITH: VERY SEXY, AND THERE'S THAT DYNAMITE BACK STORY WITH CALUM BEST.

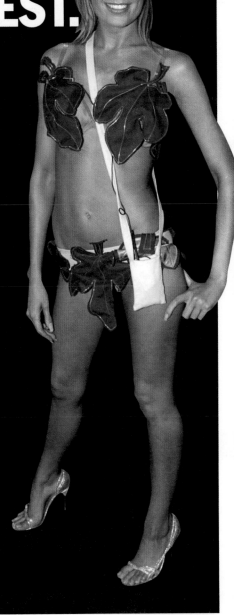

ld've gone in semi-naked, not in uit. We love nudity. The emates are incredibly savvy t holding stuff back or getting family and friends to sell us es and pictures, but we're not ested in just anything. And they ly have an idea how much a story orth. It'd have to be red-hot to e them any decent amount of ey. Our job is to weigh up how h stories or pictures are worth. things we're looking for, the big rs, are really big secrets from r past. Big Brother 6 is a great . My feeling is it's vintage. re's only been one day without an ment so far. They all know what 're doing. Based on their antics far, the most interesting people the tabloids are Saskia and well. She's as bankable as a Big her housemate gets. There's the our angle – you'll get great shots of her. If Orlaith stays, she's great e. Very sexy, and there's that amite back story with Calum . Other than that I love Makosi,

very confident and aware of her sexuality. She knows what she's doing. She'll be great for pics and quotes. There are housemates who are interesting but not very bankable, like Kemal and Derek. I don't think our readers would empathize with them, but they'd be amused by them. Of least interest? I can't see anyone buying up Science or Craig for a scoop. Anthony could probably do gay mags but there wouldn't be much money in them for him. That said, the show has been beautifully cast this year. A lot of extremely interesting factions have emerged and the stories haven't stopped coming. This is one of my favourites so far. I love it.'

chapter six

WEEK 06

WEEK 06:
Unrequited Love

By Maxwell's eviction on Friday night, the accidental star of Week Six had almost provoked my first Big Brother tear of this year's game: it occurred while I was watching Craig with a new and ill-suiting skinhead, slightly drunk, highly emotional at the loss of his buddy, suddenly back inextricably in the bosom of Vanessa – the first of the many friends he had worked through in the house – dancing around to Christina Aguilera's 'Fighter'. 'This is in my top ten! Ever!' he called out to his dancing partner, before throwing some robust and, well, interesting shapes on the dance floor to the diva's invocation to be a stronger

person starting from within. This was how far Craig had come in the house. This was how far he had spiralled downwards. I mean, everyone knows that 'Fighter' isn't even in the top ten tracks from *Stripped*, its parent album. The boy was in serious need of some help by the end of Week Six. He had endured a full Big Brother breakdown. Both the week's and one of the game's most fascinating narratives was peaking. Who, what and, indeed, *why* is Craig?

Where do we begin?

The week opened already riddled with pathos, with the young hairdresser affronted at the brass neck of Orlaith for offering to make Anthony a lowly cup of tea. Beneath this quivering, char-shaped dilemma lurked the more pressing and fundamental fact that Craig had fallen hook, line and sinker in love with Anthony – or at least appeared to have done so from the other side of the Big Brother glass – hence his 'I am the bitch' outburst, only days earlier. The two were bonding splendidly, complicated marginally by the fact that Anthony had never socialized with an openly gay person before in his life – 'I think that Maxwell's better adapted at that sort of thing because he's worked in Top Shop' – and that Craig himself had not yet quite come to terms with defining his own sexuality (despite his eyes lighting up when Maxwell jokingly offered to service him orally later in the week – 'Now you're talking my language!'). As Maxwell and Saskia played out their own romance with such personable theatricality, the remaining team members had found themselves doing a spot of shadow dancing in the background, only one of them oblivious to the other's motives.

Now, the keener Big Brother eye could've spotted beneath this a relevant incident from as early as Week Two, when Craig was beginning to

Anthony had never socialized with an openly gay person before in his life – 'I think that Maxwell's better adapted at that sort of thing because he's worked in Top Shop.'

let his waspish humour unfold into the house. He had speculated to Vanessa about Anthony's sexuality, with one cow-eye cocked at the muscled and bronzed beefcake, half sneering, half susceptible. A friend of young Craig's had told him before he entered the house how to spot a gay boy. If you ask them what they would do if they ended up sharing a bed with one of their same-sex friends and they flounder with the answer, THEY ARE DEFINITELY GAY. Perhaps wishfully, Craig had asked Anthony this very question, and, although any reasonable person could observe that the young lad's response – 'I dunno, like' – was more in the vein of 'What is this relative stranger doing asking me about my sleeping habits when I hardly know them?' than 'Yes I am, in fact, a deeply closeted homosexual', Craig had curled his lip and raised his eyebrow as if uncovering a long-suppressed truth. There was no one better in the house for that curtain-twitching, dinner-lady sneer than Craig. Moreover, from that moment on he trailed Anthony with a fascination bordering on the morose, until their friendship blossomed as it had to as a matter of some urgency once the other core members of their gang had left the building.

> 'Can I touch your boob?' asked Anthony, politely, in the manner of one asking to borrow a tenner.
> 'You can suck it if you like,' replied Orlaith.

Craig's confused state of mind regarding matters of the flesh was not likely to be helped in any way by what would lovingly come to be known in tabloidese as 'the pool orgy'. On the evening of day 37 the housemates' emotions were heightened by the mini task in which they – most successfully Derek and Eugene – had had to shed collectively a teaspoonful of tears. The Big Brother house was rewarded with a slap-up dinner. They were informed that they must all wear an approximation of black tie, and they scrubbed up very nicely thank you. 'It's like taking the staff out for their Christmas lunch,' observed Derek, manfully straddling that gap between absolute scathing contempt and unfettered admiration in the way that only he could do (Derek, it should be added, was by now a television genius and had the most banners come Friday's eviction).

Perhaps emboldened by Saskia and Maxwell's earlier undercover romps or perhaps out of sheer and simple frustration, Makosi kicked off a relative sex-fest for pudding. Throughout, she kept her diamante necklace on. A very cute touch. Brandishing her bosoms at the newly available and – top marks here, kid – surprisingly strong and resourceful Maxwell, she jumped into the pool and stripped off her bikini.

Orlaith and Kemal soon joined her. Anthony was last in. It was clear something immense was happening when Orlaith's response to a full tongue sandwich with the by now tumescent young stripling was for him to have a couple of sucks on her beloved new breasts.

'Can I touch your boob?' asked Anthony, politely, in the manner of one asking to borrow a tenner.

'You can suck it if you like,' replied Orlaith, politely, in the manner of one giving him a hundred. He sucked away. Then Orlaith and Makosi snogged, as if to fulfil every Geordie boy's fantasy in one fell swoop. Anthony bobbed up and down in the water. Makosi again complemented him on his ample manhood. ('Vanessa, you would need stitches!' she later commented on the same subject, fast becoming a favourite and hardly harming the lad with the viewing public.)

After a while, Orlaith tired of Anthony's furtive nuzzles. 'You've had enough sucks, now,' she ordered, like some wartime matron dishing out her rations. Makosi was quickly back in full vixen throttle, though, and would later announce that Anthony had made her climax with his finger and impregnated her, in an act of defiance of both science (but not Science!) and nature. Whatever the weather, someone was having fun underwater and mostly it was Makosi. Anthony followed instructions vigorously and to the letter – a fine, if drunken student.

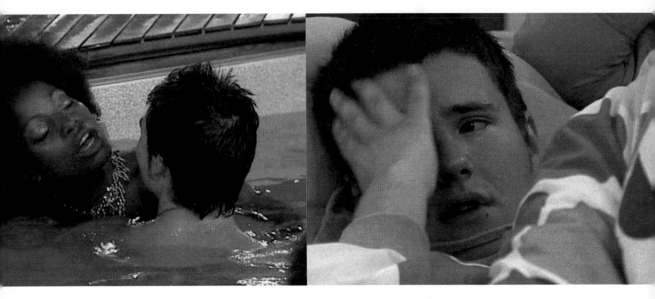

Kemal looked on, trying to enjoy things, but was left for dust by the two foxy madams and their Geordie toy. Maxwell looked appalled from behind the showers. Eugene looked flummoxed, as ever. Science looked, slyly, a little intrigued. Vanessa looked absolutely delighted, though sensibly stayed away from carnal matters (what with them not involving sweets, or anything). And Craig? Craig stropped off into the kitchen to find solace and comfort in the fatherly figure of Derek.

'I shouldn't be such a twat,' he said, tearfully eyeing the pool shenanigans revolving around Anthony. 'I must have something written all over my face that says "treat me like shit". No matter what I do for people, it's never enough.' Derek gently comforted the boy through his moment of unreciprocated ardour and wiped away the tears of a story that is known all too well to many gay boys and their friends. He was turning into a nice sort, Derek, through all this. He later told Big Brother, in the diary room: 'I think the innocence of youth is eating away at him. It's unrequited love and there's nothing more hurtful than that.' Trying to enter into the spirit of it all, Craig leapt into the pool and was soundly kissed by Orlaith. The lack of chemistry was tangible.

The morning after the night before proved uncomfortable for some. Anthony and Makosi

'If,' she retorted, by now a little melancholy, 'there's a camera in the pool then I'm not f✳✳ked because we didn't f✳✳k.'

swapped 'what happened there?'s in the kitchen at 6.30 in the morning, looking for a glass of water. But it was quite clear what had happened. One sniff of the barmaid's apron and Anthony was anybody's. Makosi denied sex. 'Everyone else thinks we shagged but we didn't. I said he fingered me and I came but that was it,' she told Orlaith.

Anthony was less analytical with his pals. 'Did I make a complete prick of myself last night or what?'

Science tackled Makosi in the bedroom: 'If there's a camera in that pool then you're f★★ked!'

'If,' she retorted, by now a little melancholy, 'there's a camera in the pool then I'm not f★★ked because we didn't f★★k.'

As ever, Anthony brought it back to how he would be perceived from the outside. 'Women will be disgusted with us.' Perhaps mindful that it is mainly women who comprise the text vote, he added: 'Stupid Geordie idiot.'

Maxwell didn't help his own popularity by coming over all censorious aunt, perhaps feeling a little that his own and Saskia's thunder had been stolen. 'I hope your mothers are proud of you this morning,' he muttered. Come now, Maxwell Widdecombe!

As it happened, Anthony escaped public nomination by one lucky vote. By the time the holiday camp task was in full swing and nominations were uncovered, it was Science versus Maxwell. The two – sworn but mutedly respectful enemies – fought a slow but admirable battle. 'May the best man win,' uttered Maxwell, as the nominations were announced. 'Likewise, man,' said Science, from behind a rather doomed smile. Science evidently thought he was off.

'I'm the person that he dislikes the most and he's the person that I dislike the most,' said Maxwell in the diary room. Science had his own axe to grind to Big Brother: 'Maxwell is ignorant beyond a pig eating his own faeces. He doesn't like me. I don't like him.'

Maxwell was making every attempt to swing into full cockney swagger, perhaps mindful of Saskia's advice to him to keep his pecker up. He and his chums shaved their heads on the night of day 41, in return for some booze and a bit of a television moment. His perceived confidence in his own ability to win, not just against Science but the game outright, didn't go down well with the audience as message boards rallied around for Science, not so much as fans, more as a vote of defiance against the London lad.

The other bookies' favourite also began to show alarming signs of losing the plot and her early lead in Week Six. Makosi's announcement – tactical, impractical, whatever! – of her possible impregnation was a fantasy too far. She was by now beginning to look just a little bit crazy. 'I think I will have it,' she confessed to Kemal and Vanessa in the loft. 'I have been quite broody already for the last six or seven months. Children are gifts from God. Whatever happened in that pool happened. You can imagine a child with Anthony's eyes and my hair.' Of course, the viewers all knew that Makosi was sporting a weave. Gotcha.

On day 41 a mass debate was staged in support of Maxwell and Science's causes. Again, Craig put himself bang in the middle of matters when his beloved Maxwell (his attentions had shifted since Anthony had betrayed him for a fake breast in the swimming pool) failed to pick him for his team, favouring Derek instead. It wasn't personal, of course, but the slightest touch could now send Craig over. Derek, an esteemed political speech-writer, served Maxwell up a proud speech in his honour and proved him right to have selected him all along. But Craig diva-stropped into the loft. More tears. More angst.

Which in many ways is how we ended up with a lonely figure dancing to a lesser Christina Aguilera track as Maxwell was chucked out of the house on a 57–43 per cent margin. The cockney looked flabbergasted at the result, but his astonishment was nothing to that of Science, whose I AM AN ICON t-shirt was given momentary significance. Yet no one could be more shocked than Craig, now left with only a stray heterosexual chum to buffer his dazzling confusion. For a very brief moment I wanted him to win the game. For with a major player gone and one beginning to look as if she had lost the plot, it was truly anyone's trophy by now. Why not Craig's?

Just remember, kid. You are beautiful. No matter what they say.

Profile:
MAXWELL
Trotter Ward

AGE: 24
STAR SIGN: Aquarius
HOME: London
JOB: Engineer

FIRST IMPRESSIONS: It's Peter Kay on the Atkins diet. In a Hackney t-shirt? Can't be right. Has that high street hairdo that all boys have now, bit spiky out the back, a bit mullety. I think we may be witnessing the lad contingent. Does a good whoop and holler with the crowd. Lot of confidence, life and soul. Promising.

Maxwell is 24 years old and 6 foot 2: 'a proper streak of piss'. Prior to Big Brother he was living with his dad in Islington and working as a maintenance engineer for the retail chain that owns Top Shop. He trained for four years as an engineer and then went to Faliraki on holiday, where he ended up staying for two seasons. On his return he worked the tills in Top Man before changing over to the maintenance side of things. 'You get home at three in the afternoon and the money doubles so I had one year on the tills, one on the tools.' He has two sisters, one older and one younger. His little sister cried on the phone when he called her after getting out. He says he was always in 'the wrong crowd' as a kid. He has only had three proper relationships, of which the longest one lasted for 'about a year'. He thought he was in love at the time, but says that was because he was only 17. Maxwell values his sense of humour above all else, but says that he is not even 'the funny one' in his immediate group of friends. His first love is Arsenal. He goes to every game his team plays. He prefers a bar to a club – 'It's easier to have a chat in a bar. I'm rubbish at dancing – but his favourite music is funky house. He has no idea what he'll be doing in ten years, 'apart from watching the football with a beer. I never usually know what I'll be doing in ten minutes.' Maxwell's hero is Ian Wright because 'he's a proper Arsenal boy'.

I meet Maxwell in the Big Brother studios two days after his eviction. He's much taller and skinnier than you expect him to be, and both warm and friendly. He hasn't had a newspaper front cover but he has signed a management deal in tandem with Saskia. He seems a bit more laissez-faire about all this, less ambitious for the prizes that being in the show might throw up. He is genuinely easy-going. I wonder whether this will affect any future relationship he might have with Saskia, for whom all that seemed to matter so much. That said, he's spent most of his time with her since his eviction and says things are going well.

The question I guess we should ask is why are you here?
I know. I've had everyone coming up to me in the street and saying 'you're really funny'.

Would you agree that everyone seems to be very canny at the game this year?
Yeah, I would. I went on the show to have a good time. That was it. Pulling a nice little bird was a bonus. But I wanted to enjoy myself, maybe make a couple of new pals and that ...

There was no technique at all?
I tried to be extra funny. I was trying to be ten out of ten all the time. I don't think the house will be as funny now.

Why do you think the producers wanted you?
Bit of a cheeky chappy, bit of a geezer, likes his beer and his birds and his football. I thought that was it, bang on.

You looked flabbergasted to be thrown out on Friday. Do you think that your confidence played against you?
Yeah, maybe, but I also think there was a bit of game-playing from people coming up to me and saying, 'You're definitely going to be in here on Friday.' Derek told me I had nothing to worry about and I think he did it so people outside would think I was a bit cocky.

You've been one of the guinea pigs in the house – testing the camera runs and stuff – before, haven't you?
Yeah, twice. I've done two or three days a couple of times. I was on standby last year but they put Becky in, which I'm glad about. It's never very nice being the last one in, apart from maybe this year for Orlaith. She's looking pretty strong.

Were those catchphrases of yours meant to catch on?
What like 'off the hook' and 'f**k about'? I didn't think everyone would be saying them outside but it was good.

I think one reason people didn't really believe your relationship with Saskia was real is that – no offence – she does seem way out of your league. Is she the fittest girl you've ever kissed?
Yeah, she is. I'm not being funny but I only ever have a girlfriend when they're absolutely top. I'm not the type of boy that needs to be going out with someone all the time.

Do you think that relationships that strike up in the house, like Helen and Paul's, tend to stay the distance because of the intensity of it all?
Maybe. You also want to give it a go because you've been in there together. But I still can't believe that Saskia would want to knock about with me. I've proper landed on me feet.

When you first got into the house, were you eyeing the others up as competition?
No, not one bit. Right at the beginning I thought that Kemal would be loved by the public for running around in stilettos and showering in the bin and shit. They love an oddball, don't they? Then the appeal sort of wore off with him. I don't think he could keep it up.

Have you followed what's happened in the house since you got out?
No. Not interested, to be honest. I'll watch bits and pieces, like evictions. It'll be weird. Craig said to me that the only thing that bothers him about being in there is that he doesn't get to watch it. I'm not like that.

Have you made lifelong mates in there?
Yes, I have.

You seemed to spring to life a bit more when Saskia left. She was properly wearing the trousers the week before.
I know, but I just melt away for the right bird. I'm a proper cheeseball. I'm not embarrassed about it, though.

Did Kemal's comment about the magazine deal hurt as much as it looked like it did?
No. At the end of the day I knew she was up for eviction and I wanted to get me nuts in. That was it. And it didn't work.

Were you not tempted at all to join in the pool affair?
Not one chance. If I like a bird then I like her. I'm pretty loyal. Makosi and Orlaith didn't interest me one bit.

Who will win Big Brother 6?
Absolutely no idea. It's an open field, mate. To be honest, I'd like Craig to win. Anthony doesn't need the self-esteem. He's a lovely fellow, Craig.

Evicted

Evicted

Evicted

Mary 01 WEEK

Lesley 02 WEEK

Sam

Eviction Night

Evicted

Roberto 04 WEEK

Evicted

Saskia 05 WEEK

Evicted

Maxwell 06 WEEK

BEHIND THE MIRRORS IN THE HOUSE

BB FEATURE

WEEK 06

In the middle of Big Brother 6 I am taken behind the scenes of the house itself, to inspect the damage, watch the housemates and see how they are recorded 24 hours a day. The blackened-out passageway that goes round the house is known as the camera run.

Ben Hardy, one of the senior reality directors, greets me outside. As we hand in our mobile phones to the two security guards manning the Portakabin that acts as the back entrance to the house, it couldn't be more thrilling. We have chosen our moment well and all the remaining housemates are in the living room in a rare moment of togetherness (actually they are giving each other evil sideways glances, but such is the nature of the game this year).

Being in the passageway circumnavigating the house is one of the most disquieting experiences a Big Brother fan can have. It feels like a mixture of watching a silent movie,

sneaking a look over your neighbour's fence and waltzing round a swishy film set. It is also like looking at old friends. I can second-guess when Craig is going to put his hand over his mouth in mock horror – which he does. Watching Makosi fiddle with her weave has a comforting level of familiarity now. Obviously, I've met expelled housemates at this point, but watching them interacting – life-size! – under the powerful night-time telly floodlights, which must give them an odd sense of their own peculiar position, is fascinating.

There are always at least five cameramen and women working 24 hours around the clock in here, as well as the numerous cameras tracking movements in the house. From behind each mirror – and there are loads of them – you can see into the house. Patrick's design comes vividly to life and the house suddenly turns from being a jolly place where the housemates live into a technical extravaganza. Ben

comments on how good the design has been for the cameramen to work with this year. There are triangular nooks that jut into the rooms and when you walk into them it is as if you are standing in the house. At one point I am about a foot away from Makosi in the living room. I take care not to sneeze. And yes, the carpet is absolutely filthy.

This is how Big Brother comes to feel so intimate. Through the amazing televisual technology you can be in the house with the housemates, tracking their every move. Privacy does have its place, however, and it's nice to see there's a padlock on a removable panel over the toilet mirrors. Ben explains that they're only used for absolute emergencies or for the secret viewings from the toilet into the diary room.

The camera run is as close as you can get to being in there, short of running across the lawn. You're at ear-flicking distance. Ace.

chapter seven

WEEK 07

Let's be frank here. By rights, on previous form, a clear winner should have emerged by now. A fully formed front-runner. Somebody showing leadership qualities. Someone the bookies handle with caution. Somebody who has captured the imagination of a nation, got the message boards buzzing. But no. Everyone was fair game. Loyalties and affections were split. Today's choice became tomorrow's laughing stock. Nothing at this stage in the Big Brother 6 house was certain, least of all a winner. A prime time to start really messing things up.

WEEK 07:

Deceptive BB6

Big Brother is watching you

This was just one of the brilliant side effects of cramming the house full of its most diverse and strong characters yet; Big Brother 6 was going to be fought right down to the wire. By the end of Week Seven, Derek's observation in the living room – 'They say that a week is a long time in politics, but a day is an even longer time in the Big Brother house' – was proving to be apt beyond measure.

Buoyed by his triumph against Maxwell, Science had taken a strong position within the group. Eugene's predilection for interrogating everything with the minutest, nerdiest of detailing had made him strong in Internet communities and forums. Anthony's streak ahead in the 'manpoints' battle after his shagger-pool shenanigans had got the everybloke vote. Kemal was still a fascination, of sorts, though his stilettos trick was to sour. Derek's ability to lend everything a narrator's touch of genius – 'There's more mince in that walk than in the entire freezer,' he commented to Kemal as he strutted into the living room in a thong – would be rewarded with plenty of public affection. Craig's ongoing, unrequited love for Anthony had become the defining tryst of the house now that Saskia and Maxwell were both dust.

So all the boys were still swinging (some more so than others, natch). What was becoming clear was that Week Seven was not going to be a good one for the girls.

On day 42, a shift occurred that would lend a new texture to many relationships in the house and would even affect relationships with the house itself. After Kemal won the hilarious 'answer the question before' mini-task, wearing a brain machine and glasses ('because clever people wear glasses'), he gifted the house with video messages from their friends and family.

'There's more mince in that walk than in the entire freezer.'

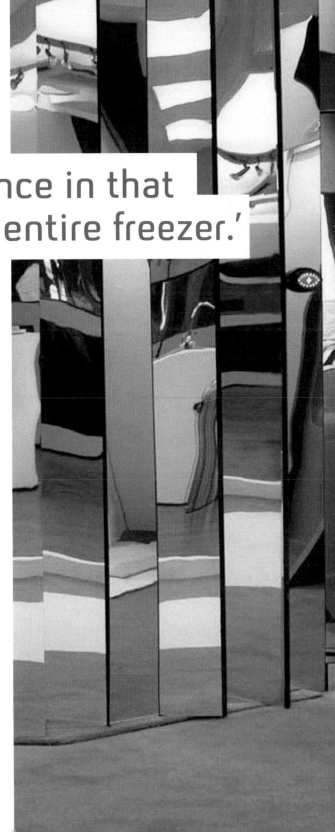

Suddenly the real world came looming in. This was a sharp reminder that people were, indeed, watching on the outside. Though much had been performed with the cameras in mind, the beauty of Big Brother is that much had not, and it was surely these unselfconscious moments of anger, tears, madness, and the curious house habit of rubbing one's own nipples in a circular direction, that went running through every housemate's mind as they were confronted with their nearest and dearest.

Everyone's messages were sweet. Anthony's nan looked nice. Craig's mum and dad alluded to the Anthony 'affair' and his mum made a moving speech about a mother's love being unconditional. 'They know!' said Craig to Anthony in the garden, referring for once directly to his own sexuality. It was a moment. Craig's story was complete. Vanessa asked Makosi if she thought her mum looked like her. 'No,' replied Makosi. 'She's prettier.' Kazam! Derek had a triumvirate of white women proclaiming his loveliness, prompting speculation from Makosi that he might be their butler. Science's dad implored his son to 'keep it scientific', which warranted a nod of approval from Eugene. 'I think your dad looks like a really cool person.' Eugene was turning out to be a nice guy, see, though still finding it difficult to actually connect with anyone. Orlaith had a blub at her family sitting in their sitting room, and Makosi worried that her sister not wishing her well may be indicative of some sort of disapproval over the pool orgy. She cried, too, later in the diary room, confessing to Big Brother: 'Usually I can put a silver lining to every cloud, but there is a lot I have to deal with when I get out and this … I don't think I can deal with.' In the event she vented her quiet spleen on Kemal and temporarily signed her own popularity's death certificate.

Given that he had won everyone their video messages, it seemed appropriate that Kemal's family should play the blinder, reducing him five minutes later to a jibbering wreck in the bedroom and incurring tears of genuine empathy from Derek, who would confess later that it reminded him of his own coming out. Craig withered, looking slightly trumped. For in Kemal's message his family, too, said that they supported him no matter what and were very much enjoying his antics in the house. They looked and sounded like lovely, intelligent people. They didn't turn out anything hysterical. It was just poignant. In a way, it was the end to Kemal's story, too. Stiletto-strutting defiance in the face of disapproval looks brave. Jackie-O-sunglasses-sporting defiance in the face of approval looks slightly daft. Though on

a personal level his message was lovely, it may well have cost him the game. A surreptitious question entered the head of every Big Brother watcher. What mattered more to Kemal: personal happiness or popularity? And the Big Brother voter can be a surprisingly moral beast. Badness is always punished, selfishness always transparent. Those days of showering in a dustbin seemed an eternity away as he took to his bed for three days' convalescence.

Makosi, Orlaith and Vanessa were quick to acknowledge Kemal's change of fortune in one of their bitchier sessions in the loft. The girls had been tiring of Kemal's shtick for three weeks now and every time Makosi insisted to the boy's face of her love, it was sounding less and less convinced. By day 46 she was ready to vocalize her views on him. 'I think he's changed since his parents did the video because his story ever since he got here was "Oh, my parents don't love me …" Now he can't dramatize his exit.' Orlaith was quick to grasp the concept. 'Oh, so now the public will see that he isn't shunned by his parents.' Makosi welcomed the co-conspirator. 'Ever since that video was shown he's been in bed. He doesn't do the lipstick any more. He doesn't do the stilettos any more. He doesn't do the zshushing any more. He doesn't do the "baby doll" any more.' It was harsh, but true.

But, again, it was the backhanded delivery which meant that she, Makosi, would be punished for her observations.

Ever the empress, even of a crumbling empire, Makosi's crown had begun to tarnish. She was starting to look weird and manipulative. And matters were being driven further into the mire. On day 45 a note had been left for the house. 'Housemates, Big Brother will lie to you twice this week. You guys are amazing. Big Brother XX.'

The lies were to be: 1) that nominations this week were optional; and 2) that the housemates Big Brother announced were up for eviction were the correct housemates.

Big Brother instructed them in the voting scheme. They could nominate in the diary room *if they wished*. It caused mayhem. Most housemates felt, with wobbly conviction, that the optional nominations weren't a lie. Only Anthony, Craig and Kemal nominated, and in so doing unknowingly exempted themselves from the public vote, though Kemal further alienated himself from his friendship group by refusing to tell them whether he had nominated or not – perhaps not wanting to admit to having Judas-kissed Makosi.

On day 46 they were told their second lie: that it was these three nominators who faced the

public vote. The distractions in the face of this announcement by Big Brother were good and plentiful. There was a treasure hunt, which everyone thought was a lie until a bit of formation gold-digging – another thing the housemates were good at – led to Anthony finding the treasure and scooping new manpoints. ('My hero!' squealed Craig, sweetly.) There was an Olympics task that performed the twin triumph of making the TV programme nice and timely – London had scooped the Olympics this week from right beneath Paris's nose – and showing everyone's bulges beneath some particularly unforgiving Lycra. Though she had continued with her pregnancy ruse ('I did not come here to have a baby. If Posh and Becks could call their baby Brooklyn because he was conceived there, what am I going to call mine? Big Brother Jacuzzi?'), Makosi made sterling work of the rhythmic gymnastics with Derek.

But from here on in everything was a countdown to Friday's live eviction and the dramatic denouement. By now used to their pack facing weekly evictions, Anthony and Craig handled their supposed nominations manfully. They contented themselves with a new game in the swimming pool that appeared to simulate front-entry anal sex. Nice. Kemal handled the news with less grace. He did a lot of talking in the diary room, becoming slightly obsessed by the idea of Makosi as a mole or an actress working on Big Brother's behalf. 'It is killing me on the inside. Makosi is not who she says she is.' When Big Brother scribbled in lipstick on the shower mirror, 'There is a mole in the house', it only confirmed the poor boy's suspicion and he sat outside the diary room, whispering under his breath: 'It is Makosi! It is Makosi!'

Yet he still couldn't let go of Makosi and Vanessa. He joined in with the girls' bitching of Orlaith. 'Madam is trying to take over,' said Makosi of her pretty 'friend'. But it was the straight-talking Irish girl, a little older than the rest, who best handled the week's double-bluffing. She recognized it as a part of a wider picture and in the loft she bravely let slip her thoughts in front of Vanessa, Makosi and Kemal. 'Friends can be very, very bitchy. Yous have been here for seven weeks. It's not a lifetime. Yous have got to remember as well that everyone is in here to play a game. Yous aren't in here because you wanted to make new friends. At the end of the day everyone is out for themselves. You can say that you aren't but everyone is. There is a big prize at the end of this. £100,000 is a lot of money. Don't yous forget it.'

'Friends can be very, very bitchy. Yous have been here for seven weeks. It's not a lifetime.'

Madam should probably be allowed to take over. She was fresher to the game, a little less warped by it. Orlaith was quietly quite cool in Week Seven.

It was Vanessa who would end up the week's victim. By the time the group had gathered in the living room to hear who was to be evicted, every conspiracy theory and configuration of the Big Brother lies had been speculated upon. And then they were told. Vanessa looked shaky at best as Davina imparted the news. She retired to the toilets to get herself together but composure escaped her for the rest of the evening. The group sat round the dining table to hear the results of the public vote. The two least popular were Vanessa and Makosi (Makosi got an astonishing 47 per cent compared to Vanessa's meagre 26 per cent) and for one of them the game was over. Everyone's on-the-spot nomination of Vanessa – apart from a still odd-looking Kemal – was a formality and made rather uncomfortable viewing.

The outside world had been unfair to Vanessa. She was a good conduit for the inner machinations of the mind of Makosi. In rooms full of shameless popularity-mongers, she could often be heard with an insightful remark.

Most of all, Makosi looked devastated. She cried in the diary room later after both she and Vanessa had been booed. 'I feed from being loved,' she said, wiping a tear from her eye. 'Knowing that the public don't want me on the screen has ruined the experience for me.'

Profile:

VANESSA
Layton-MacIntosh

AGE: 19
STAR SIGN: Leo
HOME: London
JOB: Student

FIRST IMPRESSIONS: Could this be the house screamer? Got that look about her. Pretty, nice confident walk. Very familiar Big Brother type: she's gonna make a beeline straight for the gay boys, basically. Shoulder to cry on. Ear to hear you. That kind of idea.

Vanessa Layton-MacIntosh is 19 years old and lives with her family in Croydon. Before entering the Big Brother house, Vanessa was a sales assistant at Carphone Warehouse and Claire's Accessories in Croydon. She was also studying Business Management and Accounting and shared a house with five other girls, but being a bit of a family girl she split her time between that house and home. Vanessa was a big fan of Big Brother before she went in and still maintains the love. She says that it is 'one of those things that not many people get to do in life. I think it's amazing. And the moment I was picked I was so delighted to go into it.' Vanessa auditioned in London and was an instant hit with producers. 'I don't know what they saw in me. Good question, but at that time I was very bright and bubbly and I do love to be the centre of attention.' She says that her auditions were among the times she has felt most confident in her life, but still she was surprised when she got into the house. Her favourite colour, famously, is pink. 'I don't even know what it is that I like about pink; there is just something that makes you feel better about seeing the colour.' Her other favourite thing is cookies. Vanessa says she doesn't have a hero, as such – 'Though my dad is up there' – but she does, like most of the other housemates this year, have a special place in her heart for Christina Aguilera. 'Very ballsy woman,' she says, before adding sweetly that Makosi was her hero in the house.

On the Tuesday after her eviction, I meet Vanessa at the hotel she's been put up in post-Big Brother. It's no secret that Vanessa has taken the whole experience the hardest out of all the housemates so far, but she's an absolute delight and her vulnerability is quite refreshing, and makes everyone else seem a bit hard-nosed. It doesn't express itself quietly either: she's an erudite, fluent and talkative girl. Any game plan she may have had obviously went straight out of the window when she got in the house – living there was a bit of a struggle. I think everyone was a bit much for her, bless her. She's steadily getting back to normal. She looks so pleased to be out.

Has it all been a bit much for you, pet?
It was hard. Much harder than I thought it would be.

Do you regret it at all?
No, everything I do I see as a life experience and I'm so glad I did it. But, yes, it was a lot harder than I expected it to be. Actually, coming out now, the more I talk about it with people, the better I understand what was going on in there. Outside of the house I am usually a confident, loud, bubbly person, and for the first time in my life I've gone into a situation where I've been the quiet one. It was strange, but obviously they were all a lot stronger personalities than me and at times that can be very hard to deal with. Saskia and Maxwell were really intimidating. They just seemed to strut round with this confidence that they'd be there until the last week. They behaved like they had a lot of power in the house. There were a lot of huge characters in there, playing the game really hard, fighting for attention. There was a certain amount of falseness for the cameras, which starts getting on your nerves.

What did you expect to get out of the experience?
Probably to get along with more people. In general I thought it would be a lot more fun.

Are you pleased you stayed in seven weeks?
Yeah, I am. I think that's fantastic. I'm very proud of how long I lasted. There were a lot of times I wanted to go. But I'm not a quitter.

Good on you. Did you have a game plan?
No, no, no! I thought there were elements of my character that would contribute well, if that's a game plan? I do like a bitch and a gossip.

Was it a lot more bitchy and gossipy than you expected?
Yeah. Which I love about the show! I think when Saskia and Maxwell went I contributed a lot more. I felt a lot

more confident when they left. But even the ones who are nice – like Science is essentially a really nice guy – they are difficult to live with. It's weird when it's 24 hours a day. A couple of hours of Science you'd love. He is a nice person. But he could pick an argument with the table. And Craig and Lesley were really close in Week One. Team Britney. Things change very quickly in that house. Alliances don't last.

Have you learnt stuff in there?
Oh yeah! I've learnt a lot about myself. I'm stronger than I thought. I've dealt with a lot of issues in there. Low times, low self-esteem, having to compete for attention with others, having trust broken, losing friends. I felt totally betrayed by Craig running off with Saskia to stir it up. He completely ignored me when she was in the room.

How do you feel about the way you were evicted?
Yeah, brilliant TV. Harsh exit.

Makosi really looked after you, didn't she?
She was like an older sister. She was amazing. When I moved from sharing a bed with Craig at the far end to sleeping near Makosi, that was the first time that I felt comfortable. I felt really, really at home with her. She made me feel better about myself and more confident.

What was the pool orgy like from the inside?
Strange. I mean, oh, my god! One minute we were all giggling and having a laugh and the next minute they were all pulling each other. One thing led to another. Me and Kemal got straight out when they started taking things to another level.

What advice would you give to someone who wanted to go in the house next year?
I'd still advise them to go in. I'd say go for it. You don't know what to expect and that's the fun of Big Brother. You go in there taking a risk and you learn a lot about yourself. Go for it.

Have you watched any Big Brother since you've been out?
I've watched snippets. I saw a bit of the show last night. I haven't gone through my stuff.

Are you going to?
Yeah. All I've seen so far are bad press cuttings and it does your head in. But I do feel like I've kept my self-respect.

Who is going to win Big Brother 6?
I'd say Derek or Anthony. Obviously I'd love it to be Makosi and I think she was favourite to win for a long time but people change day by day.

HOW TO BE A BB HOUSEMATE!

BB FEATURE

WEEK 07

In the interests of finding out a bit more about how to become a Big Brother housemate, I tripped along to the Endemol offices in West London to ask Creative Director Phil Edgar-Jones what it is the producers are looking for. Here's what he said.

1 Housemates all want the same thing: recognition. 'It's a myth that housemates are any more savvy now about Big Brother than they were in the beginning. They are self-selecting because the motivation is always the same. They come to us. We don't go to them. The levels of intervention from us increase as the show progresses – we have to find creative ways of making the experience different – but the housemates' motivation is always the same. They want to be famous.'

2 The producers aren't looking for 'types'. 'This year has been gayer and more ethnic than ever before, but that hasn't been deliberate. We don't look for certain people in order to tick boxes. It just so happens that if you have been marginalized in some way then you will probably have more layers to unravel than other people. The worst Big Brother contestant is a one-dimensional one.'

3 Sometimes you just know who will work in the house. 'Charisma is absolutely indefinable. Basically, we took one look at Derek and said, "OK, he's in."'

4 The producers don't make decisions based on intelligence. 'We don't say, "We want a house full of thickies." Of course we don't. Just as we don't say we want intelligent housemates, either. This year there are a lot of clever people in the house, for one reason or another. But we've had clever people before. Shell and Stuart were both very clever last year. PJ was a very bright lad. I think the difference this year is that the housemates haven't been scared of being clever. They haven't tried to dumb down. It does seem to be cool to be clever in the house this year.'

5 The most popular housemates with viewers tend to be the ones who are a) the nicest and b) the closest to themselves. 'That's what viewers seem to want. Realness. They are a very sophisticated audience, the Big Brother audience, and very moral. They reward good behaviour and punish bad behaviour. We know that we have to surrender a lot of control to the housemates to let them tell their stories but sometimes they are astonishing. Makosi has been amazing this series. When Kemal was convinced she was a mole we actually had a production meeting in which all the executives asked each other, "Did you tell her to act like a mole?" She's had us at times.'

7 Housemates must be prepared to relinquish control of their lives. 'In some ways, Big Brother as a character is very much like a parent, though we've made him a wittier one this year. There is something regressive about going under his jurisdiction. Having housemates is like having five-year-old children. They rely on Big Brother to feed them and entertain them.'

8 The best Big Brother housemate will just be him or herself. 'We can spot a fake in five minutes.'

9 Your past is who you are. 'This is the stuff we're interested in. Your opinions on current events, your love life, your politics, your sexual preferences, your jobs, what you do for fun. It can be about the answers you give to questions or the way you answer them. It could be the way you are with the executives or the way you behave with a runner that gets you in. There are no hard and fast rules, other than it has to be about you.'

6 A housemate should be as modern as their audience. 'Big Brother is incredibly modern in many ways. There is an old school of thinking in television that you have to be "talented" in some way to get on the telly, which has been proved to be rubbish. And who says that Little and Large were "talented" anyway? The ambition to be on television has always been there and it's always been shallow. We don't have any truck with the old guard. Which is why we can get to tell these stories that haven't been told before. The Craig story of unrequited gay love has been brilliant this year. The racial questions that have been asked are fundamental.'

10 People are complicated. 'They will always surprise you, whether it's for better or worse. People aren't just types, they aren't like this or like that. They have many, many layers. The worst thing you can do is try to be a "type".'

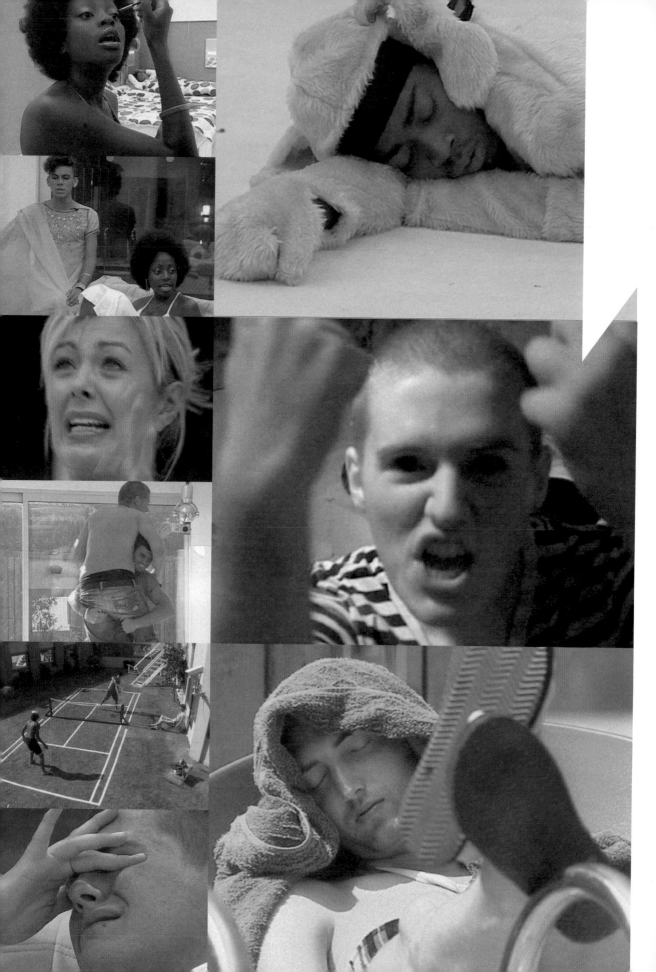

chapter eight

WEEK 08

Some time out to consider the state of mind – or what was left of their minds – of the housemates in this weirdest week in the game so far. Week Eight was a battle for everyone: their nerves shattered, their patience stretched, their tears flowing like particularly aggressive waterfalls. Those who came out the other end started to look like they really deserved that £100,000 prize. Sometimes it is tougher than you think in there.

There were those who didn't survive, of course. Notably Science, who managed to get himself ostracized by everyone, and was an

WEEK 08:

Mole/Actress?

Big Brother is
watching you

unsurprising leader for the public vote when it came to day 53's nominations. He argued and argued. He managed to fall out with Orlaith over a clothes horse – quite some feat, particularly to have included in the process the almost-perfect line: 'That thong's too far up your arse, love. As usual!' – and to provoke Derek into hatching a plan to get rid of the boy he had once spoken of with all the affection of a father towards a son. 'Just ignore the ghastly creature,' uttered Derek to the ensemble cast, who were all willing conspirators in his silent treatment. The boy may have come from the ghetto streets of Chapeltown, Leeds. But he was headed with some certainty to Coventry.

Week Eight's other public nominee, Orlaith, managed most of the week's action in tears, though she found a cunning way of keeping herself busy once it was announced that she, too, would face the public vote. 'I need to exfoliate, moisturize and do my tan. So that should keep me busy.' For four days!

Orlaith bore the unfortunate brunt of the ongoing, elliptical and weirdly expressed feud between Kemal and Makosi. By now it was clear that the early friends had jumped in too fast and too far with their expressions of love for one another. When they said 'I love you'

what they had really meant to say was 'I love your clothes and hair', as Makosi had become quick to point out. Kemal had quite obviously mistaken a temporary obsession for a love – and who can blame him: how many of us at 19 know the dark differences between what it is to be fascinated by someone and to love them? – and was beginning to look weird in the way he was expressing his feelings. He became obsessed to the point of distraction with Makosi-as-mole. He simply would not let the idea lie and for at least three days appeared to be able to talk to Derek about nothing other

'That thong's too far up your arse, love. As usual!'

than her being an actress and a spy. Compounding his weirdness was his absolute conviction that he was right, and that he was going to leave the house to be congratulated by a beaming Davina on being the one who spotted it.

Even when Eugene produced the actual mole at which Big Brother had hinted in lipstick on the mirror – a furry number buried in the beds at the side of the lawn – Kemal refused to calm down. He was looking increasingly paranoid. Taking it out on Orlaith was a little mean: in front of everyone in the living room he confronted her about talking about people behind their backs. His grand act of public spiritedness went down like a lead balloon and was delivered with all the emotional conviction of a lost shopping list. He had the wrong target, of course.

In the event, public unpopularity, evidenced in a bout of boisterous booing the preceding Friday, turned out to be the making of Makosi, who leapt back onto form and dispensed with some of the sillier lies she had been playing out for the sake of the game. No, she declared by day 52, she would not be the first housemate to become impregnated in the Big Brother house.

'I am 80 per cent happy. God knows I was not happy about this.' If only she could lose her antipathy for Kemal. Alas not. She repaid in kind his nomination of her against Vanessa the previous week. 'I feel he has – besides the fact that he's lied to me about a couple of things – he has this thing about me being an actress, which he is using against me. I can't stand the little boy. I feel he is not gay but is using the fact that a lot of people who vote are gay to win votes. He's using his sexuality as a card and he's using Makosi as a card. I can't stand the boy.' Harsh words, again.

It was Derek who, if anyone, was beginning to look like the malevolent house bitch by Week Eight. He began badly and steadily got worse. Derek was severely wrong-footed on day 51 by Anthony asking him if he had accused him, behind his back, of being gay. 'No, I didn't say that,' he lied, though he had aired his suspicions about Anthony's sexuality often and at length with most of the rest of the housemates, quite certain at one point of his closeted nature. All three of the gay housemates had at some point questioned Anthony's heterosexuality, though there is a possible psychological link between their speculations and the size of Anthony's muscles. (Sometimes it really is that simple and that wishful.)

But no. Derek denied it all and cast the blame onto Lesley, a long-departed housemate, hardly at liberty to defend herself to the Geordie chest over any intimations about his sexual preference. Worse still, Derek vaulted ahead with his denial by suggesting some form of phobia on Anthony's part – 'Would there be anything wrong with it if you were?' – though the boy had done nothing but cuddle and be fondled by Craig for some three weeks now. Hardly the behaviour of one who had a problem with his gay kith and kin. No, there was an interesting discussion there to be had and Derek leapt away from it at every turn, denying any complicity. That future in Conservative politics seemed by now pretty much assured.

Craig himself continued on his lovelorn path. His habit of continually contradicting his earlier self was becoming something of an endearing comic turn. If anyone was going to come out of

'He's using his sexuality as a card and he's using Makosi as a card. I can't stand the boy.'

the Big Brother 6 house with a newly informed knowledge of himself it would be Craig. 'I love sex!' he declared to Kemal from the comfort of his bed. 'It's a big full-on part of my life.' This directly contradicted his confession to Vanessa in Week Three that he did, in fact, hate sex and found it overrated. The reason for his newfound love of physical intimacy was never far away from his thoughts. 'I one million per cent do not fancy you,' he declared to Anthony on day 55. 'Come here and give us a snog,' he countered on day 57.

Eugene had started acting as a conduit for the thoughts of Derek much as Vanessa had for Makosi a couple of weeks earlier. But he had developed himself, too. His discovery of the mole gave him a prime chance to do one of his comedy accents. The Big Brother mole turned out to be from the West Country. Who knew? He was one of the few who felt compelled to challenge Science on his argumentative ways, though his attempts fell largely on deaf ears. He told Derek that he thought the final three would be Kemal, Anthony and Craig, and suggested Anthony as a winner, a theory that by now could be posited with some conviction.

Yet, as everyone else went steadily doolally, as they all began to show their truer colours, broken by either house rules or housemates or

house shenanigans, it was little Anthony, previously nothing more than the eye candy of the house, who strode purposefully into his own. He was the only one who seemed in full possession of a true motive. Aside from a minor gripe with Orlaith about the butter and a couple of little tiffs with Craig, he also seemed to be able to keep his temper in check. Anthony was becoming the good person in the house, emerging as a favourite. From the beginning he had made clear his hopes to win. This had never been a secret. But for now it was beginning to look like a distinct possibility. The bookies had put him at evens come the week's end. He had shown some flair where others had simply flared up.

Plus – and it is a big plus in the Big Brother world – he had put on one almighty winning show in a mini-task. When he entered the diary room on day 55 and was greeted with a fanfare for being the 2000th visitor into the room, he snipped a ribbon, drew back a curtain and found himself winning a date with Big Brother. This was how far Anthony had come. From only weeks earlier declaring himself a little uncomfortable around gay people, he camped up his date with the savvy professionalism of an old clone. He dressed in his finest finery. He chatted up Big Brother. He made lewd advances. He plucked a condom from his

pocket and wondered aloud whether it might be a bit presumptuous on their first date. He did his swift shagger motion onto the chair with a good, brisk, enviable thrust. Though his performance suggested that what he wanted all along was to be the sole man on camera – in its own way weirdly redolent of Maxwell in the workhouse task, performing for all his worth – there was something undeniably more camera-ready about Anthony, easier on the eye, and ultimately more natural and true to himself, less of a caricature.

His streaking ahead was not lost on Derek, who commented to Eugene in the pool, 'Anthony is now looking like a winner. He is ultimately a placid lad but I want people to have views and care about things.' He let it be known who he would like to see scoop the trophy. 'I think that Kemal's done a brave thing to come on this show and to be who he wants to be.'

By Friday's eviction everyone had painstakingly avoided Science. Only Makosi was defending the poor guy's corner. Big Brother asked her if she felt protective towards him. She showed surprising humility in her response. 'I don't want to feel like a surrogate mother towards Science. I know behind all that shouting there is hurt and pain. Nobody gives him a chance to understand him. I sleep next to him every night

and he has sleepless nights. I hear him tossing and turning. I hear him sneeze. I feel for him. Really.' How sharply her words contrasted with those of Derek about 'the ghastly creature'.

Science himself visited Big Brother to make his peace on eviction night, presciently predicting his departure. 'We aren't all meant to get on,' he understated wildly. 'The reason why I did all this is basically because my low income isn't enough and I want my dreams to become reality. I want to take myself to a higher level.'

When he was told he was leaving, he said to everyone, 'It's OK, people, it's time for me to go.' The wisdom of Science couldn't be left at that, though. He had more to add, poetically. 'We had good times. We had bad times. And we had in-betweeny middley times.' In the end, Science had probably been truest to himself of the whole house. He was the first person in several weeks to leave neither hysterically nor hated, nor without hugs. Beneath it all there was a silent, sometimes grudging respect for the Scientist.

It was left to Orlaith to have the final word, as she sat clutching a pillow in the living room. 'Another flipping week of shit ...' she mused, staring into the middle distance.

Profile: SCIENCE
(Kieron) Harvey

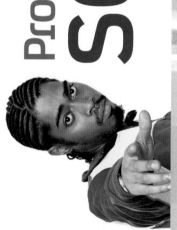

AGE: 22
STAR SIGN: Leo
HOME: Leeds
JOB: Entrepreneur

FIRST IMPRESSIONS: This one's a bit cool for Big Brother: cornrows, good rapper's gait, nice sneakers, moody face, he's well hip hop. Definitely haven't seen his type before in the house. Presenter's job on Channel U when he's finished? T-shirt says 'I AM AN ICON'. Not exactly modest then.

'Science' was born and brought up in the Chapeltown district of Leeds and is 22. He christened himself Science in 1998 when he was working on some demo tapes with friends who called themselves Fester and Dreadman. 'Don't get nothing twisted. I'm still Kieron, know what I mean?' He says that only his mum calls him Kieron still. Prior to entering the house, Science was living with his mum and two sisters in Chapeltown and holding down two jobs as a nightclub barman. He says he enjoyed this work, 'Yeah, man. Do you know what it is? At the end of the day, anything that I do then I'm going to do it 100 per cent to the best of my ability. I do everything like that.' He says that he hasn't always been confident but that it is part of becoming a man to lose your shyness, come out of yourself and stand up for yourself. Big Brother is not his first foray into the media as he has made two documentaries before for BBC Radio Leeds, one of which – *Searching For The Truth* – has won broadcasting awards. He recognizes that people are somehow drawn to him but doesn't quite know why. 'It's a tricky one. I think people are interested in outsiders, particularly if they are confident and outgoing.' Science wouldn't be bothered if being in Big Brother was the end of his fame but he will be surprised if it is. 'I don't see this as anything other than a beginning. I genuinely don't think that this will be the last you hear of Science.' Science's heroes are Marcus Garvey, Martin Luther King and Mozart.

I meet Science three days after his eviction in a café round the corner from the Radio 1 studios in London. He has just recorded an interview for *The Chris Moyles Show* and he also popped into 1Xtra to do a little stint on the urban sister station. He was ace on both. He is a compelling character and it strikes me that the producers must have thought they'd found gold dust when he auditioned for the show. He's so not a usual contestant: way more street, not even really an audience member. He talks slightly in riddles but has lots to say for himself. If you hit on a subject he likes he can go at it like the clappers. He notices all the music on the caff stereo and signs an autograph for the Italian mama behind the counter, bashfully reciting his own catchphrase: 'You get me?'

How does it feel to be out?
It feels back to life. Back to life, back to reality. Everyone's been showing me much respect. I'll tell you what, though. I need to get back to living, to get back to reading some books. Just to put stuff back into my head.

Were you a fan of the show before you went in? You look like the least Big Brother person in there.
Yeah, I watched many of them, I cannot lie. You never know what to expect with each series, that's the beauty of it. I know what you mean, though, I don't look the type.

Are you the coolest person that's ever been in there?
To tell you the truth, yes. On a certain level, yeah. Moloko had skills though, man.

I really respected you when you apologized to Kemal for throwing water at him and came out with your real name.
Thank you. I needed to do that. It was one of those moments when you realize that you are the older man. I was genuinely sorry and that's why I used my real name.

What was your strategy for being in Big Brother?
I didn't have one but I knew that I'd be myself. At the end of the day everyone can be my witness that I was not playing up to the cameras. This is the way that I am.

What do you think the producers wanted from you in there?
The truth. And that's what they got. I'm a bit loud. But I'm not as noisy as I was in the house all the time.

You aren't as aggro?
No. I don't have arguments all the time. Of course I don't, man. There are three sides to Science; I guess one will stick. I can't get on with people that are bitching you up all the time behind your back. But I could deal with those things because I did have strengths. People couldn't break me down or suss me out.

Were people trying to break you down?
Oh yeah. All the time. I don't want to go into specifics because there were times in there where I should have just laughed something off and let it go. With Orlaith in the last week, I was just washing my clothes. I should have let that one go.

Were you really chuffed to beat Maxwell?
I seriously thought I was going and I'm pleased with myself that I never ever let any of that stuff go to my head. I kept my feet firmly on the ground.

You were a lot more confident after you'd beaten him.
Yeah, but because of him there was a distance between me and Anthony that shouldn't have been there. In certain ways we're very similar. Both been brought up by our mothers, we're both working class, northern. We shouldn't have been against one another.

Did you make up little raps about people in there?
Some of them had them themselves. Lesley was the Udders from Hudders. Roberto was the Pasta Masta. Kinky Pinky [Vanessa] – she was all right. I liked everyone having nicknames.

Was it all driving you a bit doolally towards the end?
There were people winding me up. I was in there and nobody wanted to socialize with me at the end. That was hard. It's hard when your kindness is taken for weakness.

Did you last a lot longer than you expected to?
Yeah, man. I really respect people for that. I survived a few and I thought I'd go when I was up. I could see the games being played on me. I kept it real.

You weren't afraid to stand alone in there, were you?
No, man. I was not afraid to stand alone. I like standing alone when I'm surrounded by people who are concerned with the little things. And I don't attack in packs.

Roberto and Derek wanted to father you at first. How do you feel about them now?
They didn't need to father me. The Dark Deceiver [Derek] wasn't used to people of my age being interested in things. I couldn't really talk to anybody on a level. They were all obsessed with the show.

Who do you think will win the show?
The Dark Deceiver, even though he shouldn't. He might wing it.

Do you regret going in at all?
No. I enjoyed every single minute of it. It was amazing.

We spend all day laughing our heads off, telling each other that we're the luckiest people in the w

SHARON POWERS

EXECUTIVE PRODUCER

What is it about Big Brother that makes it the daddy of all reality shows?

It was the first one of them all and, in a really competitive market, I still think it's the best. The reason that Big Brother has lasted so long and why it'll continue to do so is that it's a really simple format. You get a load of housemates living in a confined space, and the viewers vote off the housemates they don't like. And that's it. It's a really simple premise. We have fun throwing in tasks and twists but ultimately it's about viewers deciding the fate of strangers in the house. It's really, really simple and I think that's why it has stood the test of time. It's a popularity contest. Or an unpopularity contest, if you like.

Is the feeling that 'it could be me' part of the appeal for the audience?

Oh, absolutely. It's a great pub conversation: would you go on it? Would you put yourself through it? What would you be like on it? I think Big Brother is about people, essentially, and the relationships between people. If you don't like people then you won't like the show. And the other way round. There is a lot of snobbery around reality TV shows but Big Brother is about human relationships.

How important is it, from your point of view, to try to keep a sense of humour backstage?

We spend all day laughing our heads off, telling each other that we're the luckiest people in the world, doing the best jobs in the world. We're coming up with daft ideas all the time. The minute somebody says 'You can't do that!' you think, OK, I'm gonna do it. We have a great time. It's really important to have a happy team.

There are a couple of preconceptions about Big Brother that probably need smashing. One is that the production team is a bit contemptuous of the housemates. What would you say to that?

Look, without the housemates, we don't have a show. Simple as that. We can come up with all the best ideas in the world, but if the housemates are no good then you haven't got a show. They are fundamental to the success of it. That's why we're so pleased to have found a great bunch of people this year. The important thing from my point of view is that people have wanted to go on a journey with them, to spend their summer with them.

How right did you get the casting this year?

I'm really chuffed with all the housemates. A lot of them have given us stuff that we weren't expecting. Before they go in, all we can do is get to know individuals, and you can never tell how 13 or so people are going to interact as a group. They're all very individual people with dominant personalities so it took ages for them to form groups. What I've loved about the dynamic this year is that as people have been evicted, the shift in friendships and alliances has changed week by week. So even when somebody goes and you think it might be a big loss, the impact on the house makes great television anyway. The casting has been pivotal. You might not have liked the people in the house as much as you have done in previous Big Brothers, but you probably want to get to know them and find out what makes them tick more than before. They're complex characters and you do want to get under their surface. Before they went in they each thought they'd be the strongest character. None of them was expecting the fight for dominance that there's been.

Somebody put it to me that you've probably had at least five winners in there this year. Does that make sense to you?

Yeah. A week's a really long time in this year's Big Brother. Makosi was hugely popular and then she went in the pool with Anthony and did whatever she did and it shifted. Then it shifted back. Eugene gained massive support when he began showing his vulnerable side. People's popularity is literally shifting daily.

Do you feel like you've inherited a national institution here?

Yes, I do. I feel really privileged being the captain of this huge ship just trying to avoid all the icebergs. All I can do is do my best with it. It's a huge responsibility.

Has it been difficult to keep a lid on the aggro this year?

No, not at all. In the first few weeks when they were fighting to be the leader of the house, they were constantly at each other's throats. They did tend to go over the same old ground, particularly about food, but we had to let what happens in the house happen. It's always much more interesting than what we try and shoehorn in there. What we started to do as producers was to say, OK, they're arguing, that's happening, but we have to try and follow the stories that are happening outside of those arguments. What we started to do in terms of telling the stories was to use the arguments as a backdrop. We followed the cliques and alliances forming. When people started to form groups then the arguments became about stuff that mattered. The story always needs to move on. Look at Anthony and Craig. What an amazing story that has

been. Craig has come out on national TV and his absolute adoration of Anthony and how Anthony is coping with that is just beautiful and so full of texture.

Another preconception that could do with smashing is that the housemates somehow don't know what they're getting into.

They totally know. What was interesting in the audition process was talking to potential housemates about whether they had a game plan. Loads of them had. The housemates realize that it's up to them as much as us to make the show a success. That's come from watching housemates in previous years. It's brilliant, probably at its best, when the housemates decide independently to entertain the viewers, which has happened a lot this year.

Do you think that collectively this year's housemates are the most naked Big Brother housemates in terms of their ambitions?

Yes, I do. They don't hold back. Where we've seen this has been in nominations. In previous years it's been a struggle for Big Brother to establish the real reasons that people are nominating others. This year you can't shut them up. The nominations have been one of the highlights of the show. Kemal and Derek couldn't wait to spill the beans. Everyone's been great at nominating.

Do you think that Big Brother has changed the nature of celebrity?

Yes, it has. I don't think that celebrity itself is all it's cracked up to be. When we were auditioning housemates we were very clear about the downsides of having a little bit of notoriety for a short length of time. Going on Big Brother is not a fast track to your own TV show or endless millions. That just does not happen. I think that over the last few years there have been maybe a hundred housemates in there and, of them, only Brian, Jade, Nadia and possibly a few others have got a career out of it. We impress on people that they have to think about why they're doing it and what they're expecting to get out of it. If you're expecting fame and fortune you'll be disappointed. If you go on Big Brother, you've almost certainly got more currency while you're in the house than when you're out. I don't think that going into the Big Brother house is anything you should take lightly, but we make sure that anyone who does want to go in knows the cons as well as the pros of it.

Is the key to being a successful Big Brother housemate not to try to win it?

I don't know. But one of the interesting things this year has been how the housemates have responded to the crowd's reaction when Davina's talking to the house. In many ways that's been people's downfall. It seemed to be the start of the end of Saskia and Maxwell when they heard the cheers. Those who thought they were popular have seemed to change the way they behave.

How would you sum up Big Brother 6?

This has been a Big Brother of extremes. We've had romance, unrequited love, bullying, fall-outs, enemies coming together, shock evictions, and we've had it all played out by these brilliant, massive characters. I'd say it was the best Big Brother yet, but then I'm biased, aren't I?

chapter nine

WEEK 09

Perhaps inevitably, given Science's unique propensity to create friction (Science friction, natch), his exit led to a temporary change in the mood of the house from tough to tender. Perhaps even more inevitably, given the remaining housemates' unique motivation – mostly self-interest – well, it didn't last. Not that there weren't some genuinely lovely moments on the way. Nudged along by some inspired production work behind the scenes, Week Nine was as close as they had yet come to being a harmonious group working alongside one another for the greater good. For all of, ooh, five minutes?

WEEK 09:
Obsessions

Big Brother is
watching you

Bearing in mind that even the great friendship of the series was reaching an unfortunate, mirror-held-up-to-themselves impasse, the omens for a loving week were not good. Yes, even Craig and Anthony had kicked off the week with one of a growing number of tiffs on the orange sofas. With a hangover, Anthony declared illuminatingly to Big Brother on day 59, 'When Craig's had a drink, maybe he thinks a little bit too much of us.' He paused for thought, before consolidating this bit of psychological insight. 'Maybe he's a bit obsessed.' Craig put the matter blunter, in his own unique pattern of succinct Craig-speak. 'I should be f**king sectioned when I get out of this place.' Haven't we all been there?

The first attempt to inject a little love into the house partially backfired. Possibly because it had been put into the hands of Orlaith, fast becoming the house's collective hate figure now that Science had gone to the urban university in the sky. Nonetheless, the Irish beauty was given a secret mission by Big Brother – her first – which involved a love buzzer.

She was told that every time the buzzer buzzed she had to hug the housemate closest to her, pay them a compliment and tell them she loved them. Makosi, with a sense that could only be referred to by now as 'seventh', scuppered her mission within 20 seconds. Orlaith ran into the diary room for advice and came out brandishing a new tale: that because she had told them she wanted to leave the house – a mantra she would repeat tirelessly for the rest of the week – Big Brother had provided her with a buzzer to get her into the diary room every time she was in trouble. Ingenious, eh? Amazingly, the rest of the housemates actually bought her crazy-ass idea.

Makosi looked a little nonplussed. Perhaps out of a moment of kindness to Orlaith, though, she

'I should be f**king sectioned when I get out of this place.'

let it go. Before long, the blonde lovely was telling both Craig and Anthony of her love for them, under Big Brother's benevolent instruction. It was one of the few things that would keep the girl from going crazy for her remaining time in the house, and did seem to stand her in better stead with the boys on the orange sofas, who had embraced her almost as one of their own by the time it came for her to leave. But still she bore the brunt of much of the house anguish. If there is one thing more guaranteed to cement unpopularity among Big Brother housemates than being clever, it is being beautiful.

Later that evening, Craig cried to himself for a moment in the pool. His knight in shining armour arrived to soothe some of the pain, though he was, alas, largely the cause of it. Anthony jumped manfully into the pool. 'I'm going to put some of my good mood into you. I'm putting it in you,' he declared, quite blissfully unaware of what he was saying. A light flashed across Craig's brow, then dimmed. 'It's not going in.'

On day 60, a second production attempt to lighten the atmosphere in the house was markedly more successful. A positivity-themed game of pass the parcel led to some shared appreciation. Ironically, it was Orlaith's instruction to pay everyone a compliment that was delivered with the most sincerity and charm. She even managed a few touchingly nice

'If you walk down any High Street in any city anywhere in this country, you will find 100 Anthonys. You will also find 100 Saskias. You will find 100 Maxwells. You will find no Kemals.'

words about Derek, a move she would no doubt come to rue by the week's end. Oddly, somewhere within this love-in, Makosi managed to share the news with the assembled group that she had had an abortion. It silenced the crowd for a moment, before Derek interrupted with the gayest response in the history of responses to such a revelation. 'Had you thought of a name for it?'

In keeping with the new mood of intimacy being fostered in the house, the nominations in Week Nine were not to be for who you wanted to leave, but for who you would most like to save from the public vote, and here the great lost relationship of the series began to rear its head. Anthony voted to keep Makosi and Makosi voted to keep Anthony. It was difficult not to speculate at this point how they might get on outside of the artificially intense relationship of the house. Clearly there was a lot of affection there. More so than in Anthony's perfunctory nomination of Craig, which sounded more like an obligation than a genuine request. 'We've passed the sexual stuff,' said Anthony of Makosi, but there was still a glint in his eye. Had Makosi, too, made the wrong friendship alignment? Had she chosen the easy gay man with whom she could talk hair and outfits over the true object of her affections, an object who would

possibly show her vulnerability (a card she was resolutely not going to play in the house)? Sometimes it is the unresolved, even undeveloped relationships in the Big Brother house that are the most fascinating.

That Makosi didn't choose to save Kemal was no longer a surprise. She had tired of her plaything, though they bonded in the by-now ceaseless attack on Orlaith. It was the flamboyant Turk who would join Orlaith in the public vote. Not since Maxwell's second public nomination against Science had there been a more mutual, unspoken house conclusion as to who would stay. And not since Maxwell would there be a wronger one.

But Kemal flew back into his own in Week Nine. Big Brother put his suspicions about Makosi as mole to rest in the middle of the spy task, but true to his extravagantly analytical nature, Kemal had sorta worked this out for himself. No, what refreshed Kemal in Week Nine was the lighter mood. He seemed to be settling into his role. He loved leading the spy task, and you could not help but speculate whether, if he had had Makosi's secret mission in Week One, or maybe even had had the pirate ship to captain, he might have emerged the natural star of the show and winner of the game. There was something of unfulfilled

promise about Kemal, and while his brain was clearly light-years ahead of most, his intuition could let him down. After his nuclear fall-out with Makosi, Derek was the wrong choice, though Derek was loyal to the last to his young charge. With Makosi, Kemal never seemed to get to the nub of what they were actually arguing about.

Yet for all his missed potential, Kemal would go away from Big Brother 6 remembered. And he delivered, in his bravura performance at the press conference after his eviction, one of the clearest truths yet spoken by an alumnus of the house. Informed by a member of the tabloid media that Anthony was by now the bookies' evens favourite to win, he said: 'Well, good luck to him. Anthony is a nice boy. And he wants to win. Very much. If people want him to win, then let him win. The public should decide. But I will tell you this. If you walk down any High Street in any city anywhere in this country, you will find 100 Anthonys. You will also find 100 Saskias. You will find 100 Maxwells. You will find no Kemals.' This was delivered in a cool, mesmerizing lilt, neither bitterly nor with malice. It was hyped but there was a softness to it. Was this simple wisdom beyond his years and testament to his own originality? Or was it simply that Kemal, allowed to be centre of attention, left to blossom (and freed from the

gargantuan shadow of Makosi) would have won any other year's Big Brother? As Derek put it, in his request to save Kemal from nomination: 'Although he walks as though he's got no balls, he's got more balls than all the heterosexual men in the house.'

As it was, he left on a high. The weekly mini-task to split into three groups and express the housemates' stories through performance art was a pleasure to watch. Derek encouraged Eugene and Orlaith in a tremendous mime. Craig and Kemal's song was genius. As a reward for passing the task, they were offered fags and booze or a cute kitten to play with. Shockingly, they chose the kitty, though again it was left to Kemal to provide the killer line to Big Brother in the diary room about the puss. 'Everyone's got game plans in this house, even the kitten. I'm going to nominate him next week.' Alas, he wouldn't get the chance.

Kemal's commanding of the spy task was masterful, as the housemates were introduced to the finer points of espionage in a variety of splendid disguises. Anthony upset Craig by telling him that he looked like 'that woman that died in prison' in his wig. Everyone picked up on the Myra Hindley reference. Particularly Craig. 'That is f**king disgusting. I don't want to look like a f**king child killer.' Which was

fair enough, really, but would lead to another bout of tears later. When it was announced who was nominated, Craig sighed with a new shade of torment and delivered the Norma Desmond line of the series: 'I wish my name was up there. I've got nothing left to give the public. I've got nothing left to give 'em!'

On day 62 there was an ambassadors' ball for the collective spies, in which they all developed secret identities. A further classic Big Brother moment ensued, as Anthony quietly and quickly drank himself into a stupor and Craig desperately seized his chance. He was all over the poor boy like a bad rash, squeezing him, cuddling him, 'nursing' him, to everyone's bemusement and bewilderment. 'I must not leave him,' he told them. 'He needs me!' Things developed swiftly. 'Anthony, you are being sick on me,' ran Craig's crazed commentary. 'Anthony, you are sitting in your own vomit!' Then later: 'Do you know what? I love you so much. I can't leave him. I can't leave him.' A very drunken Anthony in a pair of lurid yellow underpants attempted to escape his attentions. Eugene supplied a lone voice of sense amid the madness. 'I think I have established the problem,' he told the rest of the housemates. 'I think that he is smothering him.' When Anthony finally retired to bed,

'I feel like Winston Churchill,' he said, delighted.

escaping his obsessor, Makosi bid him good night. Anthony opened the sheets and beckoned her in with a wry smile. She passed on the offer, but looked delighted.

The next day, as Anthony's hangover kicked in, Craig told the object of his affections, 'God, they seem to be making out that I smothered you or something.' It was an unfortunate echo of Eugene from the night before. Derek managed to escape most of Craig's performance by being whisked off to a secret room to spend the night after being incorrectly identified as a double agent. 'I feel like Winston Churchill,' he said, delighted.

Kemal's eviction was greeted with appalled looks of shock and awe all round. Not least of all by Orlaith, who had by now decided that she would definitely like to leave. 'That bitch ain't walking anywhere apart from the bathroom to put more moisturizer on,' noted Kemal in his press conference.

Again, his intuition had failed him …

Profile:

KEMAL

Shahin

AGE: 19
STAR SIGN: Scorpio
HOME: London
JOB: Student

FIRST IMPRESSIONS: OK, this is one absolutely astonishing individual. He's working a look that is somewhere intergender, wearing a sari, striking poses. Incredible face. Fearless. Charging ahead. Not making a single bit of eye contact with the crowd. Totally working it. Is it drag? He definitely has that strut, but with a more curious tone. Love him.

Kemal was born and bred in north London. He is 19 years old and prior to entering the house was a first-year English Literature student at Liverpool JMU. He says his family – Mum, Dad and little brother – are all strong characters. 'I wasn't coached into standing out but I was certainly encouraged.' He says he went to a 'bad' state school but made sure that he did all right out of it. Kemal described himself at the auditions as being a very competitive person but said he never thought of Big Brother as being like an ordinary competition. He was concerned at the audition stages that the producers would not understand him. 'I was worried that they would see the diva thing only. I mean, I can be as two-dimensional as the next person. But they completely grasped the whole thing about me.' Kemal shops mostly on the High Street, in men's shops, women's and – because of his slight frame – children's. He also loves charity shops, something that he and Makosi didn't agree on in the house. He calls himself 'contemporary Muslim on the verge of transitioning to Buddhism'. He gets religion, totally, but isn't absolutely sure of his beliefs. His favourite song is 'Viva La Diva' by Dana International. Big Brother is not his first reality TV experience. If you study the *Pop Idol* archive you will see him in the last 100 of the Michelle McManus year. Kemal says his heroes are Martin Luther King, Gandhi, Nelson Mandela, Madonna and Christina Aguilera. Isn't everyone's?

I meet Kemal two days after his eviction up at the Big Brother studios at Elstree. He is enormously popular with production staff and wading through a million hellos. He has an almost regal air of exuberant dignity and is wearing a brilliant outfit of pedal-pushers, stilettos, belted turquoise turtleneck and a huge brooch. He is not fashion exactly, but he personifies style. He's also instantly captivating, though it is a little draining trying to keep up with the rapid-fire speed of his mind. He is such a product of the celebrity age it is almost disquieting: he is absolutely oven-ready for fame.

Honestly, was your dressing up anything to do with Nadia winning last year's show?
No, but her name was mentioned to me a couple of times in the house. I think that was just based on sexuality and on the gender issues. Nadia was a very inoffensive person. She wasn't argumentative and she kept quiet about things.

She wasn't an intellectual, either. You were a hugely contradictory and confusing, if brilliant, housemate. Listen, Nadia was amazing. She had that slightly different thing going on, which I have, but she had it in the right quantity. I was too extreme for people. When I got out of the car and struck a pose in a sari, I knew people would think, 'Who does that think it is?' I knew they would pick up on the arrogance. It was a show, that entrance. I don't do predictable.

The signals you were throwing out just by stepping out of that car were probably the most complex of any Big Brother entrant, ever.
The thing is, the more of this series you have, the more we know what it's about. Maxwell and Saskia knew they had more currency as a couple. Which is why I said that thing about the magazine deal. I'm proud of saying that. I was never scared of being up for nomination.

Were you afraid you were being upstaged by Makosi at all?
When I first walked in, only. She threw me for a second. There could have been a Whitney/Mariah situation, as I said, but that would've worked on telly for only a couple of weeks. It was more interesting for us to get along.

You seemed intensely paranoid by the time the whole mole business came into play. Did you feel like you'd made the wrong decision, being friends for the sake of the show?
It wasn't for the sake of the show. Her friendship was and is very important to me. Look, I'm human. I wasn't ashamed about coming out in there. I was always true to

how I felt. I knew I was an odd mix: there's the diva thing but there's a bit of an intellect and a bit of naivety mixed with bitchiness and a bit of admiration for Makosi. There was a lot going on there.

Where does your fearlessness come from?
I wouldn't call myself purely fearless. I can be paranoid as well. Makosi is what I would define as fearless. She did not care. She was very in control – though she had insecurities.

Were you upset that Orlaith beat you?
Yes! On one level, she wanted to go so she should have gone. Why waste your 50p on someone who's going to walk? In hindsight I can see quite clearly what has happened, but yes, I didn't want to go. It's no secret. But I saw it more as a TV show than a competition. It wasn't something I had to win, but it was something I had to be remembered for. I've come out at a nice point. It's not about ranking and competition. I think Anthony would rather come fourth than fifth. Of course it doesn't make a difference.

Do you ever get brain ache from everything that's going on up there?
No, I don't confuse intellect with analysis, but I do overanalyse. I could be more refined as a person by getting rid of some of that analysis. The good side of this, though, is that as much as I overanalyse other people, I also do it to myself. Not in a paranoid, oh-my-god-I-don't-want-to-be-like-this way, but I am interested in the way I work, too. The one thing I had in my pocket going into an environment like that was that I know myself very, very well. The mistake Makosi made with me – the only one – was assuming that she knew me like the back of her hand. I am as complex as she is.

Do you want her to win?
[pauses] Yeah. Because no matter what's happened between me and Makosi, I know she's been brilliant entertainment. I know the show wouldn't be the show without a character like that. I know she will be remembered as Big Brother 6 in a way I hope I will be, too.

Had you fashioned your coming-out to be your Big Brother story?
Absolutely not. Not in any way, shape or form. I didn't want that to be the big thing about me. One: I'd decided to tell my parents before I went in, but in the end I just couldn't do it, it was too messy. Two, I thought that story had been told before. I don't do what's been done before. Other people have come out in the show. A gay guy had won before, right? Bob, Jim, Brian? Brian! And there was Craig in there, anyway. No. Gay: boring. I just wanted to be open about it.

Do you regret telling your sex-in-a-skip story on camera?
No! I don't regret anything.

Profile:

ORLAITH
McAllister

AGE: 26
STAR SIGN: Taurus
HOME: Belfast
JOB: Model

FIRST IMPRESSIONS: Well, clearly she's beautiful. Stick thin, great body, toned, gorgeous face, bleached blonde. She's carrying the fig-leaf outfit with a surprising amount of dignity. Cheeky smile. Could be a bit rude. Saskia will be seething!

Orlaith is 26 years old and comes from Belfast. Two weeks before entering the Big Brother house she came to London for a friend's birthday party and decided to stay. Prior to that she was living at home with her parents. She is the second of five sisters. Orlaith says that she was bullied at primary school and that she was quite quiet as a teenager. She can't properly remember when she blossomed into the frankly gorgeous creature she is now and is genuinely rather shy at taking the compliment. She went to college in Belfast to do an HND in Business Studies and transferred to Wolverhampton for a year to top it up to degree level. This was the only time she had lived away from Ireland and a family – she lived for a three-and-a-half-year spell with a boyfriend's family – and she confesses in a giggly but slightly embarrassed tone that she has never paid a bill. The big change in Orlaith's life came, she says, when she entered the Miss Northern Ireland beauty pageant in 1999 and came second (that year was won by Blue Peter presenter Zoe Salmon, who is Orlaith's best friend). From that moment on she has earned her pocket money from modelling. As we know from the Big Brother house, Orlaith is immensely proud of her clinically augmented breasts. 'They are my wee babies,' she says, laughing. She also had a relationship of sorts with Calum Best, though she is a little sketchy on the details, after she met him at the Apartment Bar in Belfast. They are still in nominal touch. 'He's a friend.' Orlaith says she doesn't have time for heroes, but speaks very, very highly of her mum and dad.

I meet Orlaith two days after her exit from the house. In less than 48 hours she has signed a brilliant management deal and done shoots for *FHM*, *Zoo*, the *Sun* and the *News of the World*. She is stunningly beautiful and absolutely cover-ready. She's the most naked of all the housemates yet about the show and she isn't afraid to slag people off. Before I met her, Orlaith's unwillingness to play the game made me think she may have been using Big Brother as a platform to greater things but she has none of the professional savvy that Saskia exuded in her interview. Orlaith says she's a bit lazy about her career and that seems to explain a lot. She's a nice girl, basically, but, perhaps wary of their currency outside the house, no housemate ever likes a pretty girl on the inside (it's a game rule).

Saturday saw your big exit from the house, when did you decide that you were going to walk?
On the night of Vanessa's eviction. Three weeks ago. Anthony and Craig kept me positive and kept me in but from that night I'd decided I had to go. Makosi had been so two-faced.

Were you scared of an audience being there? Did you want to bypass all that business?
I knew not to do an eviction night. I came in on Week Five. I didn't really deserve an eviction night. I came in in a different way and I had to leave in a different way.

Was Big Brother a platform to get you somewhere else? I mean, you are gorgeous.
Thank you. I mean, anything after the Big Brother experience is a bonus. I wasn't leaving to do anything else other than go and see my family.

What did you want out of Big Brother?
At the audition in Dublin, I said I wanted a relaxing summer break in Big Brother.

My god, the irony! What on earth was going through your head to think it would be that?
I don't know. Oh my goodness. Relaxing! It was crazy! I'm telling you, every time I walked into a room there was Makosi, Derek, Kemal or Eugene talking about me or cold-shouldering me. It's quite hard to deal with that 24 hours a day. Derek made me feel so inadequate, he bullied me. Kemal just hated me. But you know I punked Kemal big style.

By watching him get evicted before you left?
Exactly. You have to understand that he thought – they all thought – that I was lying and I'd stay and they just stared at me with those eyes and I thought, hmm, I'll watch you go, then we'll see who's lying.

You actively wanted to scupper his eviction weekend?
Yeah! I had every intention of doing that. Basically, when I got out of the house and they showed me all my press clippings and I did the big exclusive with the *News of the World?* Yeah, I punked the guy big style.

Did you enjoy any of your time in the house?
Don't get me wrong, I loved it. The good outweighed the bad. If I stayed any longer, though, I would've ended up walking out and straight into the Priory. I would've lost my head. Och, I'm happy and I can't thank Big Brother enough.

Do you think that people will feel you didn't play the game by not letting them decide your fate?
No. They won't lose any viewers from me going. And I would've ended up in a mental institution if I'd stayed. Even after I'd left I was looking in the mirror in the hotel bedroom, thinking, oh my god, is there a camera behind that? It does play with your head.

What about your famous breasts?
My god, they are famous, aren't they? I'm surprised they were that popular. But you know what? I think it's amazing. All this publicity for a little old pair of boobs. Great stuff.

And the pool orgy?
Anthony isn't a good kisser. Makosi was better. He just didn't do anything for me, even when he was touching and sucking my boobs. He put his hands down there [indicates her groin] but I moved them away. No. Lovely guy, but no. Vanessa played it cool that night. I had a lot of time for her. What Makosi did that night in there she has to live with. It's her business.

Do you think Makosi's playing the game too hard?
Yes, I do. She was threatened by me, too.

Was the house more bonkers than you expected?
Yeah, but in a good way. Everyone who stops me in the street has said it's been brilliant and a really good year. People seem to be really captivated by it. Happy days.

Who's going to win?
Anthony, maybe? I'd absolutely love it to be Kinga, though. That would be a perfect ending for me. I'm glad she's in the house. My daddy said the way she was left in that secret garden in a bundle crying was heartbreaking. Good on her.

Can you imagine Makosi and Derek's face if she won!
Brilliant. And Eugene? That guy deserves nothing. He plays on his weakness like a wee boy. He's got the whole nerd thing worked out; he knows what he's doing. He knows.

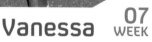

Evicted

Evicted

Vanessa **07** WEEK

Science WEEK

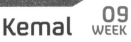

Kemal **09** WEEK

Orlaith **09** WEEK

THE TASK TEAM

BB FEATURE
WEEK 09

Now, you may think that the Big Brother tasks are just an excuse to dress the housemates up in ridiculous costumes and get a cheap visual gag at their expense. But – ha! – you'd be wrong. There are eleven people working full time on the tasks, headed by Karl Warner (weekly tasks) and Danny Bell (Saturday and mini tasks). The Task Team is a perky central force in the backstage world of Big Brother, and the tasks themselves have become an integral part of the Big Brother experience.

'To a certain extent, they help to drive the show,' explains Karl. 'Since the Channel 4 show has become that bit longer, they work as a good narrative to frame it.' Being central to the success of the show has meant the tasks have become bigger and grander, though this can manifest itself simply in the size of the emotional reaction a task gets from the housemates. 'Basically,' continues Karl, 'with a task you are looking to disconcert the housemates and challenge them in some way. Tasks have to be revealing. They need to act as a conduit to the real person beneath the agenda they've gone into the house with and the mask they want to project.'

It's a challenge for the Task Team, too, and never more so than this year. 'Because the group is so divided,' says Danny, 'you can't work on the assumption that splitting them up and putting in imaginary hierarchies will get the best results, which is the way that tasks have worked in the past. With this lot, the hierarchies and factions are in place already. What's harder is to get them to work together for a common goal. It pushes you into thinking of new and interesting ways of getting a reaction from them. They don't need to be divided and conquered. They've done all that themselves.'

When the task team start throwing ideas around, they have a checklist of objectives to be fulfilled (Is it funny? Does it reveal character? etc) and they won't leave a task or present it to the executives until it has reached their own exacting standards. Karl is particularly proud of the workhouse and the Olympics tasks this year, and it is safe to say that Danny was delighted, nay astonished, with what happened in the boxes task. 'We soon realized what was going to work with this lot,' says Karl. 'They weren't very good at concentrating for a long time on something. If a task was spread over three days they'd lose interest by day two, so we shortened the tasks. And having them lose a task for not wearing uniforms, like with the early ones – the pirates and the A&E – does not make brilliant telly.'

'So,' continues Danny, 'you keep them brief and to an exact point. That's why I've enjoyed the one-day tasks like the crying task and the counting one.'

'When we did the workhouse,' says Karl, 'it was a great relief to find something that they were collectively really good at. Like being deceitful.'

If there is one part of their work that Danny and Karl are both really proud of this year, it is in tailoring the tasks to the housemates. 'We knew that Eugene would like the spy task,' says Karl, 'with the morse code and stuff. We weren't seeing enough of him at that point.' As the viewers' relationship with the housemates has become more intimate, so too has the task teams'. Both task bosses echo the sentiments of Creative Director Phil Edgar-Jones that Big Brother himself has been funnier and more irreverent this year than ever before. And they both like Executive Producer Sharon Powers's notion that 'daft rocks'. 'A task has to be funny, basically,' says Danny. 'Funny overrides everything.'

The organic process of the show is never less than dizzying to an outsider. The production staff are thinking on their feet here, and both Danny and Karl are Big Brother when their tasks are taking place (it was Danny who had the date with Anthony as Big Brother).

'Sometimes we try to be a bit too high-concept,' concedes Danny, 'and have to be held back. You can dictate a mood with something really simple in the house like the love loft speed-dating, which worked brilliantly, or the MC battles.'

So it's all go up in Task Team HQ. They can be hard, too. 'Look, we're not here to make people famous,' says Karl. 'The housemates have got to learn that. If you take yourself too seriously you will be punished by the public. The tasks are the public's revenge on the housemates, for investing so heavily in them.'

chapter ten

WEEK 10

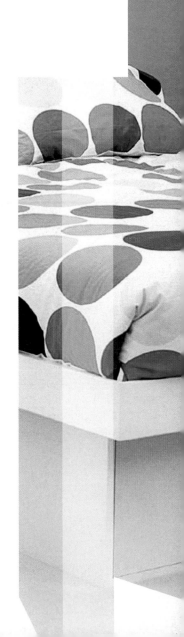

WEEK 10:
One last speech

Big Brother is
watching you

At the close of Week Ten, upon the announcement, from an ever-ebullient Davina, of his eviction, Derek Laud delivered his valedictory: a prime-ministerial, winning speech befitting of a world leader. He gathered his thoughts, cleared his throat, put on his suit jacket and addressed the throng gathered in the living room, Kinga, Makosi, Anthony and Craig, not forgetting, of course, his beloved Eugene:

'A few words from the divine himself,' he began, not strictly immodestly. 'These are the last official words that I shall speak in the Big Brother house in 2005. I've come a long way and I think that some of you know that I came here not to win it. Now you may or may not believe that. But I was here for something that I hadn't done before in travelling for 40-odd years. I was here to discover more about myself and to discover more about other people. I've been very, very lucky in my life to have had a good and honourable start and lucky enough, too, to have had some fantastic jobs. But whatever else I've done, this memory will be with me for a very, very long time and it has shaped, I hope, my future destiny. In this room there is a winner amongst you. I wish you all the very best of luck. And may all your dreams come true.'

What a fine, upstanding speech. What a way to usher in the final week of what had turned out to be *some* journey. What a generous and noble sentiment, so gracious while staring defeat squarely in the eye. Really, this should have been the defining moment of Week Ten. If only he didn't have that bloody wine bottle to contend with, eh? Talk about upstaging!

On Derek's eviction day, day 71, the devoted audience poured into the compound to cheer along their favourites and boo their villains, as per usual. The audience banners for series 6 of

Big Brother had been, thus far, frankly fantastic. 'Vanessa ate my other banner' was a favourite, to give some indication of the high concept and word play that was going on in a very buoyant and comic crowd. But while the adoring audience had been split for subject matter week in, week out, this week one theme dominated. 'Ten green bottles standing on the wall … Oh no, Kinga's sat on them all!' just about got the measure of things. This is what we call arriving with a bang.

Rewind.

'... this memory will be with me for a very, very long time and it has shaped, I hope, my future destiny.'

Week Ten began with the strains of the Clash's 'Should I Stay Or Should I Go?' being wittily piped into the bedroom as Orlaith prepared her exit (stage left) from the merry proceedings. The girl had had enough. Her permanently erect nipples were not enough to see her through. She had moisturized for the last time (um, probably not actually the last time ever, like). The previous night she had begun a campaign against Derek, telling all the housemates exactly what she thought of him, but ultimately the girl just wasn't tough enough for the Big Brother experience. True to her word, and much to the harrumphing acceptance, no doubt, of Kemal on his sofa back at home, she did one. Vamoose! She was off.

The name Orlaith wasn't mentioned much after her departure, save a couple of obligatory 'poor cows' from the ever-concerned and increasingly troubled Craig. There was a fabulously catty exchange between Makosi and Derek.

Derek: 'They said in the diary room that she had her reasons for going.'

Makosi: 'Yes. And the main one was you.'

Derek: 'Oh, good!'

Makosi put on a mourning outfit of black headscarf and Jackie O sunglasses, but who couldn't wonder whether this was in Orlaith's honour or simply because she thought that the look, like, totally rocked? (It did. Boy, could that girl work her clothes.) On the day that Orlaith left, the housemates won some toilet rolls. Perhaps in direct relation to this, Craig admitted to masturbating in the house. 'What? And shot your whack?' inquired Anthony. Apparently yes. Amazing. It would be an ongoing theme of the week. Masturbation. Not loo roll.

On day 66, somewhat presciently, Anthony quizzed Makosi about the secret garden. 'I thought that Orlaith was stronger than Kinga,' she explained to her new boys, Anthony and Craig, before turning to the latter, 'Kinga was like Lesley. You would've got along with Kinga.' Would've?!

At 9.55pm, Kinga made her way into the house for the second time, through the diary room. She wasn't suffering the indignity of sporting a selection of indiscreet fig leaves this time but, my god, were her bra straps awry. Everyone looked flummoxed by the arrival of the new girl. Some – well, Makosi – looked drained by her and she commented, 'Whoever messes with that girl is f**ked.' As if to prove Makosi's sixth sense was not failing her once again, Derek immediately began messing with Kinga, duetting on a non-specific Shakira number.

As Kinga had been put on a secret mission to appease housemates – if she could avoid a nomination by at least one housemate she would be exempt from eviction – she kept things relatively under wraps on her first night. There was a mild pool antic as she snogged both Craig and Anthony. Craig continued the unusual manifestation of his varying sexualities by licking both Makosi and Kinga's nipples. This was perhaps due to an earlier, emotional conversation with Anthony, in which Craig had confessed, 'If I won then for once in my life I would be accepted for what I am. You haven't gone through your life and had to justify yourself to every f**king person you meet. You haven't had the first f**king question that everybody asks you be about your sexuality.' Anthony rejoined with a sympathetic, 'I've been asked if I were gay loads of times.'

'If I won then for once in my life I would be accepted for what I am.'

Craig continued his accusatory tone, though. 'Have you been attacked, though? Have you been humiliated?'

Things were definitely bubbling over in that corner of the house. The nipple licking was a mere dress rehearsal for what was to come, though.

On day 67 everyone nominated for the last time. Kinga had worked her charm offensive almost too well, escaping a nomination for eviction from everyone. Singling Derek out on his Barbra Streisand card – 'I can sing to him!' – was a sweet detail. With everyone else, the house split was too much. Derek and Eugene split their votes between Makosi, Anthony and Craig and the dominant threesome stuck to the two more verbose members of the house. Makosi performed an amazing nomination ritual of doing her entire turn in the diary room with her eyes closed. Not only was it strange but strangely brilliant to boot. Derek delivered the comedy moment of the process by saying of Anthony, 'When you start vomiting in other people's houses then I really do think that it's time to think about going home.'

Freed from her charm offensive, the real Kinga was unleashed. That evening she drank a few too many glasses of wine and let her lungs do the singing. Streisand it wasn't. An infuriated Makosi was awoken from her bed with the high-pitched wail and took her quietly, but furiously, into the living room for a chat. Calmed for a matter of all of ten minutes, Kinga went in to play with the boys, out of earshot of the bedroom. It was two o'clock in the morning. And she decided to insert a wine bottle about her person. Pleasuring yourself is too kind an expression for glass, though there is a certain ingenious chutzpah to seizing the moment. Craig looked appalled but absolutely thrilled as he whooped and hollered around her. Anthony was aghast.

Warming to her audience, a by now clearly pissed Kinga ran into the middle of the lawn, lay on her back, hiked up her skirt, placed the wine bottle between her legs once more and began moaning with sheer ecstasy.

The talk, unsurprisingly, was of nothing else in the morning. 'My mum's going to think that I'm such a f**king whore,' concluded Kinga, remorsefully pouring herself a glass of water at daybreak. Later she came to explain her woes to Big Brother in the diary room. 'I did something awful yesterday, absolutely terrible with a bottle of wine. I'm so embarrassed.' Makosi attempted to elicit an apology of sorts – deliberately oblivious to her own pool antics mere weeks

earlier – with the school ma'am-ish question, 'Do you want to go and pick up the wine bottle you were using in the garden?' to the mortified girl. 'Yes,' replied a doe-eyed Kinga. 'Good girl,' finished Makosi politely, though she would later confess that the girl was sending her quite to the end of her tether, after only 48 hours in the house. Eugene offered a brotherly advice line to Kinga. 'Try not to drink so much in the future.' Very Eugene.

Maybe it was something in the water, maybe it was prompted by the new sexual revolution of Kinga, but Makosi seemed to be hinting in the pool to Anthony in Week Ten that she would reveal the whole pregnancy debacle to him. But she kept quiet. Elsewhere, in a game of everyone running circles round Anthony, Craig was finding it hard to keep his emotions quite so far from the surface. The two boys were arguing on a daily basis by now. At one point Anthony confessed, jokingly, 'I really want to kick the shit out of you,' but the joke was souring. 'You would've chinned me last night,' said Craig, after another of their multiple verbal scraps.

There was something in the relationship between Craig and Anthony now that was starting to look like it was giving a clue as to how domestic violence begins. In an argument

Craig simply could not put his finger on what he was arguing about, doubling everyone's frustration. The fact was that he wanted and needed Anthony's attention. Anthony was choosing to ignore this, perhaps wary that he had encouraged it, perhaps absolutely oblivious to everything that had gone on.

Whatever the weather, they had become too close. The promise was enough for Craig, but Anthony could not respond. By now it was clear that not only was Anthony entirely heterosexual, but also that Craig had stepped over a line and into murky waters. The two boys' overtures of friendship had clouded. Moreover, if Anthony was to win the game on the back of his reactive relationship with Craig, there was something of the Beckhams about them. Just as David gets all the public love, but without Victoria he's just a fanciable footballer, so too did the devil in Anthony's sudden popularity lie in the detail of his accomplice. Without the Craig strand to his storyline, what had Anthony actually done in the house other than be fancied by everyone (even by Big Brother!)?

At the end of the week, after Derek's eviction, things between Anthony and Craig came even closer to a head. The argument, to give the week a perfectly circular feel, was inspired by

'Do you want to go and pick up the wine bottle you were using in the garden?'

Kinga and the wine bottle episode. The newcomer had accused the boys of egging her on in her self-love. Anthony had sat mute through the accusation. Craig had been understandably miffed. But then the argument quickly descended someplace else.

Even with his place in winners' week assured – alongside reality TV's most extreme cast list to date – Craig was entering an even darker place than that wine bottle.

Profile: DEREK Laud

AGE: 42
STAR SIGN: Leo
HOME: London
JOB: Speech-writer

FIRST IMPRESSIONS: He's telly gold, right from the start. Completely unfamiliar TV type. Black, gay, posh, Tory. I mean, what on earth is he doing here? Is he on the wrong show? Did he think it was *Have I Got News For You?* There are so many questions about him straight away; can't wait to start peeling back the layers.

Derek Laud was born in London, the son of traditional Jamaican immigrant parents. He was largely brought up by friends of the family Annie and Cicely – who were on his video message beamed into the house – as his mother was between the UK and Jamaica nursing Derek's grandparents. 'They were both very formative influences on my early life.' He spent a lot of his youth in Norfolk where he developed some of his rural pursuits. His early interest in politics comes from 'the love of ideas. And argument. In the debate sense. Not in the Big Brother sense.' Little Derek would sit listening to *Today in Parliament* on Radio 4 while the other boys were out playing football. When he was 13 he wrote to Downing Street and asked them to send him a copy of the Conservative manifesto. 'Which they did, so I sat and read it and thought about it and became a member of the Conservative Party when I was 15.' He has been a Tory ever since. Derek lives in South Kensington. His friends thought he was insane to put himself forward for the Big Brother experience – 'They said, "But you can't be serious even thinking about going on this frivolous programme"' – but Derek had watched and learnt from his friend Christine Hamilton in *I'm A Celebrity, Get Me Out Of Here!* 'Now, that I couldn't do,' he says. I ask Derek who his hero is and he replies with a glint in his eye. 'Well, I've got a few. Martin Luther King, Gandhi, Thatcher and Enrique Iglesias, particularly when he's singing it.' He guffaws at his own quip.

I meet Derek two days after his eviction from the house, just as he walks off the Little Brother set. He is tiny! Neil and Christine Hamilton, the disgraced former Tatton MP and wife, latterly UK media eccentrics, are floating about, acting as his representatives. Neil makes a joke about my interviewing Derek in the toilet when he slips off for a pee. Everyone is in jolly, high spirits. Derek does a good, louche saunter and asks for someone to sort out a car for him to go and play tennis after the interview. He's easy to engage in conversation and unsurprisingly very thoughtful.

How are you feeling?
I'm feeling wonderful. I now know how Nelson Mandela must have felt when he tasted the reconnection with freedom that he didn't have for 28 years.

You've said that you were in the house to try and connect with young people in a way that you feel the Conservative Party does not any more. Did you succeed?
Many of the people in the house do not know who Margaret Thatcher is. It was interesting looking at the things that matter to them; their values and what shapes the way they think. One of the things that was very interesting to me was this constant admiration of celebrities for no other reason than they might be beautiful. I would ask what it is they've actually achieved that is admirable.

And they'd say that what they've achieved is celebrity?
Yes, of course. But that celebrity can be based on the way someone looks or the sound of their voice. These things are given by the Almighty, things over which they have no control. Why should they be so admirable?

Isn't there a bit of an irony here, that you have uncovered all of this while looking for your own fame in a reality TV show? You are now part of the Celebrity Age …
Well, absolutely. Look, the fact is that most politicians don't connect with young people and I find that astonishing since most of them are family men.

Don't you think that because of the person you are – your personality type – that you were cementing the idea that the Conservative Party are a load of crazy eccentrics?
I think that the eccentric thing is more because the Conservative Party don't seem to want any help in getting re-elected and have not a clue how to revive their electoral fortunes. I certainly don't think they're going to turn to me and I wouldn't if I were in their shoes either. Though I understand it was a young person – and I really must take her for lunch – who spent £700 of her own

money to fly the *Derek for Prime Minister* banner over the house. I Am What I Am, as the song said, and it's only a part of me that is political. There's a bigger part of me that would like to go on television purely because I believe I have made a connection with people.

Had you watched the show before?
I saw bits of the Celebrity one. I watched it whilst Jackie Stallone was in it and she was absolutely fantastic.

Were you the Jackie Stallone of this house?
I had my moments. I've never had to use plastic surgery in any way, though, and I pride myself on my ability to look after myself. There was a recycling bin in the house and everyone was asking what recycling was and what you put in it. I find that frightening.

Did anything horrify you in the house?
No. I feel that I've got a need to close differences, whether they're racial, sexual, political or generational, and I was overtly telling myself the whole time not to be an old nag. I wanted to find a way of empathizing with each and every one of them.

Is there anyone you didn't empathize with?
I think in the beginning I made connections with everyone. The person I found trickiest was actually Anthony. The reason for this was that I could not get through the self-love.

To be fair, Derek, he's a good-looking lad. Men know how to use their looks these days.
Yes, but I've been lucky enough to have much better-looking lovers than him and none of them have ever had that vanity. It was awful talking to him. He just didn't question anything. It drove me mad. And that constant looking in the mirror the whole time. Nobody else was like that until Orlaith came in. And she made him look positively modest and camera-shy.

I talked with Science about your relationship with him. We said that you would've perhaps made a better fist of your fatherly role with him if you'd had children yourself.
What an absolutely brilliant observation. I now know that I could've tackled Science in another way in the house. That is my learning experience. That's what it was all about.

Did you enjoy being in the house?
I do not regret for one minute that I did it. I would recommend people to do it, in fact. I would also recommend that they prepare themselves for it a little better than I did. Too much about life is about misunderstanding other people. It worked as a great leveller.

You want Eugene to win, don't you?
It's important that he does win. The judgements that people make should be based on what people have actually contributed to the house and not on how beautiful they are.

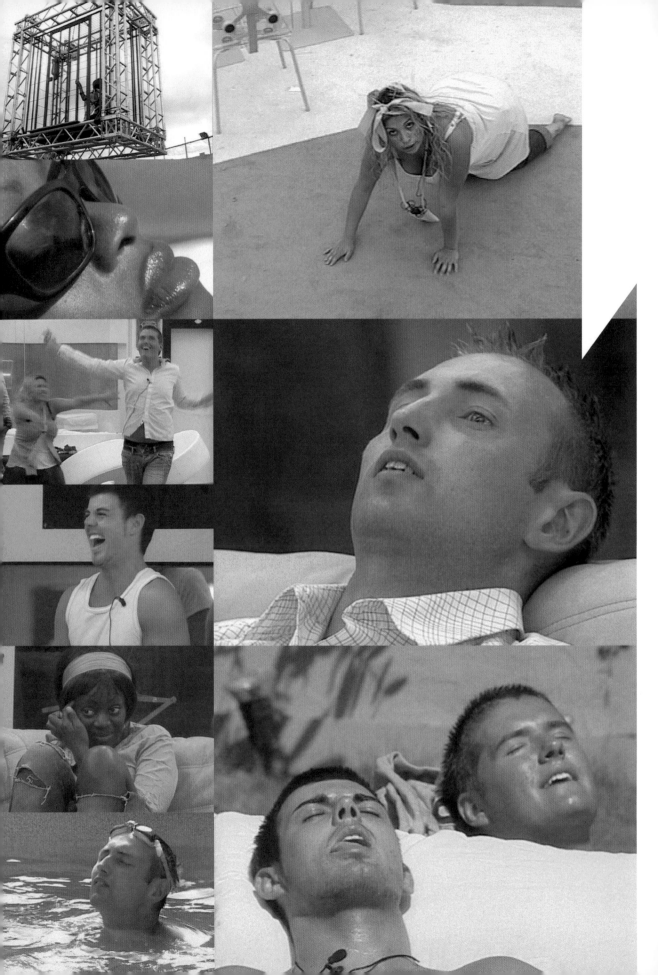

chapter eleven

WEEK 11

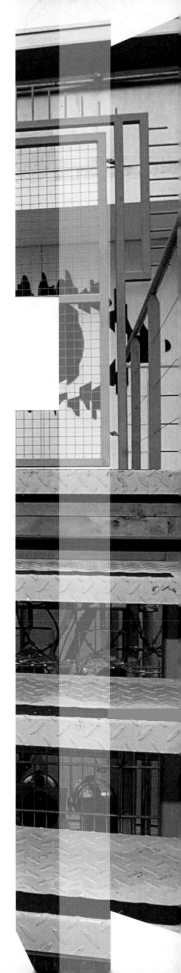

WEEK 11:
Cheque Mate

There is something, somewhat inevitably, weird about winners' week on a Big Brother. Any Big Brother. All the housemates want to get there, yet they're not quite sure what to do with it when it arrives. So really they want to get out. Which defies everything they went in there thinking in the first place. Honestly, what a tizzy!

The five left, with the noble exception of Anthony and Craig – whose friendship by now was bound by the thinnest of threads – had nothing in common. Oh, Anthony might have popped a finger into Makosi in the pool, but it's a minor detail. All the remaining competitors' favourite friendship groups had been disorientated and displaced. Eugene had only managed one friend – Derek – out of a possible nine, and he had now departed, leaving the poor boy a more quivering wreck than ever before.

By a curious mix of either staying under the radar (Anthony had faced only one public vote, and was even then afforded the luxury of a 1 in 12 chance of expulsion as everyone else faced the public vote that week too), sheer, unquantifiable luck (Vanessa had clearly saved Makosi's scalp), or the even stranger machinations of other housemates' unwillingness to play the game by the rules (Orlaith's walking meant Kinga appearing like a busty spare part in the final line-up), we were left looking like this.

Here was Eugene, complete with his tears and his joyless technical detailing of the finer points of CB radio. Here was Makosi and the remnants of her weave, which now looked like something you might find in an old hoover bag. Here was Anthony with his astonishing assortment of fitted Vivienne Westwood tailoring and carefully sculpted eyebrow topiary, still unable to spell 'pineapple'. Here was Craig and his sneer. Here was Kinga, mopping up the residual mess of being the first female Big Brother housemate to have made live masturbatory overtures to the nation. The crew could not have been more motley if Tommy Lee himself had leapt through the diary room and erected a drum kit under the showers, only to knock out the opening bars of 'Girls, Girls, Girls'. A fine time to start thinking about reflecting on the greater good of what had gone on in Big Brother 6, wouldn't you say? I mean, why not?

'Will you stay a virgin for the rest of your life?'

On day 73, the housemates were given a task that, in no uncertain terms, was attempting to bring them together and reflect upon their time in the house. Big Brother announced that the remaining housemates were to play one another, and their evicted former companions, in a play that recollected the formative moments of the game, the series, the whole caboodle (as Science might've put it). Typically, there were squabbles over who would play whom, but as their time in the house had seen blazing, stand-up arguments over everything from a clothes horse to the contents of a can of cider, this came as little surprise. Big Brother stipulated on the rule sheet that they must pick their own genre for this theatrical extravaganza. In a display of almost dizzying self-awareness, they chose the genre 'arguments', and Big Brother proved himself generous towards their understanding of what genre meant.

Eugene didn't look particularly game for all this, having previously appeared terrified by the mere sight of Kinga brandishing a condom stuffed with water by his bedside. 'Will you stay a virgin for the rest of your life?' she asked the poor lad who was feigning sleep in a foiled attempt to escape the louder house elements and collect his thoughts while reading the house rules. 'Um, I will at this rate, yes,' he

responded, comic timing finely tuned and executed to perfection.

The play went ahead, and in what can only be described as a multitextual delight (try spelling that, Anthony!), the housemates managed to distil some of their finest hours with almost spooky precision. Anthony and Craig, playing their old pals Maxwell and Saskia, frolicked under bedclothes while Makosi played Kemal and repeated a couple of his best lines verbatim: 'At least someone got wet tonight. And it wasn't Saskia,' and: 'I hope you get your magazine deal.' Anthony played Craig and Craig played Anthony as they played out, therapeutically, the boys' fight over the thrown beer. They were both jolly good as one another. Makosi was fabulous at playing Vanessa. The cruel and/or misguided might even deduce that she was better at playing Vanessa than she was at playing Makosi (outside of the house, Makosi had been the front-page tabloid scandal of the week, 'uncovered' as an actress by the *Sun*. All absolute nonsense, of course, but chiming strikingly with Creative Director Phil Edgar-Jones' assertion that at times she even had the production staff duped as to what she was doing in there).

Makosi had spent the first day of Week Eleven suspended from a crane above the house and had begun her imprisonment with a further

cracking line for the quotes of the show: 'Aha! Makosi's personality is so big they have to airlift her out of here!' But by now her habit of cementing her own legend by referring to herself in the third person was starting to get on everyone's nerves, not least of all the other housemates. 'It's all Makosi this and Makosi that,' said Craig, spotting the tic. The housemates were offered various rewards for keeping her imprisoned. Anthony took his beer. Craig hovered over a decision whether to indulge in takeaway food before plumping, quite literally, for it, and Kinga thought nothing of trading her housemate for a pack of fags, after Makosi had deliberately ignored Kinga's nicotine addiction and wiped the ciggies off the shopping list. Eugene burst into tears when faced with a cream tea and rejected it. Three words. Get a grip.

Was Eugene quite the person he had made himself out to be seemed to be the one residual ongoing dialogue the house could content itself with. By day 75 he would show his true mettle. This same day saw Craig's strangely muted exit from the house. If the surprise eviction was really a surprise to anyone – and no one had been warned – the housemates certainly acted like it wasn't.

Look, OK, I want to get something straight here. I'll get arrested for this and no one agreed

'Aha! Makosi's personality is so big they have to airlift her out of here!'

with me. But I liked Craig. There are several reasons I liked Craig and would have been happy to see him win, though by the time he exited on an absolutely paltry 4 per cent of the vote it was beyond clear that he had more chance of walking on the moon than he did of winning the game. Nonetheless, I will plough on with my controversial furrow of thought.

The reasons I liked Craig are: 1) He was the only one with a sympathetic arm for anyone when they were down (this year's housemates could be a callous bunch). 2) He told a story, a very familiar one to lots of gay men, about being in love with their best straight male friend: a story that is rarely told in fiction, absolutely solidifying my theory that Big Brother can be a groundbreaking dramatic format. 3) He was everything you want from a reality TV contestant: he was a 360-degree person. He wasn't good or bad or plain or simple. He couldn't be read in two dimensions. Everyone goes on reality TV and says they were themselves. But what they mean by this is the bits of themselves that they like. Craig? You got the whole lot. It wasn't always pleasant to watch. But it was as real as reality TV gets.

And so to Eugene. He started to emerge and show some true colours when one housemate was dramatically called into the diary room. He wandered in to be greeted by a glass suitcase of £50,000, being offered to him, just because. The other housemates watched on a plasma screen as he deliberated over taking it or leaving it for the real winner. Little did he know that once he'd entered the diary room, the other housemates had been told that if he refused the money the prize fund would double to a magnificent £200,000. But who'd leave £50,000? Honestly. Eugene didn't. He took every last penny, depriving the popular winner – very much possibly himself by this stage – of £150,000. Oh, he agonized. But watching it from behind the scenes, chucked out, Craig looked distinctly unimpressed.

'Would I have taken it? No, I wouldn't. What's fifty grand? It's a nice car. Good luck to him. It won't buy happiness.' Strangely, the rest of the housemates seemed to respect the boy for it, a rare moment for Eugene. But, really, I think I was with Craig.

Profile:
CRAIG
Coates

AGE: 20
STAR SIGN: Libra
HOME: Norfolk
JOB: Hairdresser

FIRST IMPRESSIONS: It's this year's hairdresser with a directional hairdresser's haircut. He's got that boy-band look going on, white suit jacket and jeans. After everyone else he's the first one to look like a Big Brother fan, and a Big Brother type. Looks a wee bit nervous, could be a shaky ride for him. Vile video clip of him beforehand. Surely can't be that nasty!

Craig is 20 years old and was born and brought up in Cromer, on the Norfolk coast. He is a high achiever for his age. When he left school at 16 he trained for two years with Toni and Guy, then worked with many different hairdressers before settling into managing his own salon, Saint, in his home town. Being a manager at 19 was a bit of a nightmare and meant it was all work and no play for Craig, and he's been rethinking his relationship with work while in the house. Prior to Big Brother he was living with his mum, dad and two younger brothers, Chris and Dominic, with whom he gets on really well. All of his family have given him loads of support since he left the house and they are really proud of him. Craig auditioned for the show in London and had no idea that he was doing well. He says his call from the production team came as a massive shock, and he thought he would probably only last a week or two. Craig doesn't think of himself as a confident person. 'I don't think I am confident. Everyone says I am. But I really don't see it.' He was always getting into trouble at school for talking too much and gossiping about people. He likes all sorts of music apart from drum'n'bass, hip hop and R&B. Craig says he hasn't got a hero. 'I'm not one of those people who look at celebrities and think: I want to be just like them. Because actually I only want to be me. I'm quite happy with the way I am. But I would say if a hero is someone that you look up to, then my parents are my heroes.'

I meet Craig the day after his eviction at the offices of the PR company who have been looking after him. He is surrounded by his mum, dad, best friend and our Lesley, looking very glamorous with new hair extensions. He's instantly recognizable down the corridor from that familiar cackle and, despite having slept for only half an hour, seems in tremendous spirits. He's obviously thought a lot about what went on in the house and, true to form, seems to be changing his mind about everything. Even Anthony ...

OK, since Derek left you've almost certainly been the most entertaining person in the house. Are you gutted to be out?
No, I was ready to go. I was a bit gutted Kinga and Eugene got to stay in because, to me, they aren't real housemates because they came in late. I mean, great telly, but we'd been in there since week one!

Your story really absorbed the public yet they have seemed quick to demonize you. How do you feel about that?
Do you know what? I loved everything in there. I've been portrayed as a bunny boiler but I'm not bothered by it. It's all press, isn't it? The thing with Anthony is that he's not that interesting. I've carried him a bit. And he was the same with Maxwell before that as well. I know I've been portrayed as fancying him and I will admit I did at first, but the housemates wound me up about it as well. Kinga was always going on about it. When people say I'm a bunny boiler, well, who gives a shit, really? And? Over the last three weeks the people in there have been trying to break my character down over the whole Anthony thing. I think it was orchestrated by the housemates.

Do you think people have been too quick to judge you?
I wouldn't imply that he was gay for a second but Anthony loved the attention, didn't he? Just because you're straight doesn't mean you dislike being found attractive. This is what really made me laugh. It's been perceived that I begged him to let me massage him, I begged him to speak to me. That people on the outside think I was like his dog. That just wasn't the case. You don't accidentally fall asleep on someone's lap, you know?

Do you confess that you had feelings towards him?
They're my private feelings, I don't really want to talk about that. The funny thing is that me and Maxwell were closer. He was very quick to comfort me if I was down, and Anthony wasn't. Maxwell was like an older brother, whereas Anthony was like a little brother I had to keep

looking after because he couldn't do anything. You know, I would've been the same with Lesley or Maxwell or Saskia if I'd been in with them till the end. It's just the way I am with friends. I am fiercely loyal.

You were one of the only housemates to offer people comfort when they were down.
Thank you! Thank god somebody noticed! I did it with Orlaith and I even did it with Makosi. Very few people in there were quick to defend the other housemates. It was very dog-eat-dog.

What do you think about Eugene taking the money last night?
I think it proves what he's in there for, basically. He wanted the money all along. He plays the nice guy, but he's a freak. My core ambition was just to be good value in the house. I think most other people's core ambitions were to achieve things outside of the house, after it.

You were the biggest Big Brother fan in there this year, weren't you?
Yeah. I love everything about it. I love Dermot and Davina. I was gutted I was missing it this year. I'm sure it was fabulous to watch. But everyone was trying to be certain characters. You know that Derek had that thing about being Jackie Stallone? I don't dislike the bloke but I didn't think he was right for a 42-year-old.

In the first week you said one night that you refused to compromise your integrity for popularity, then the next night you were dressed up as a schoolgirl singing Britney Spears. [mortified but guffawing] That sounds absolutely hilarious! You see, you wouldn't get that with Eugene.

What did you think of Kinga as a person? Would you agree that she was a genius choice?
I thought what she did was insane. The wine bottle was appalling, but it was hilarious to watch. I think she had in mind that the show had been really extreme this year and she wanted to take it that little bit further in the short time she was in there, and that was definitely one way of doing it. It was a way of getting herself talked about but she's got to live with it and at the end of the day I'm not sure she's going to be talked about for the right reasons now.

You know you kept on saying this was a journey of self-discovery for you? Wasn't going on live TV quite an intense way of discovering yourself?
But that for me was the best way. Chuck it in my face, get it done, everyone knows about you, that's the end of it. It was sort of a cowardly way to do it as well really because I was too frightened to tell people directly about myself.

You want Anthony to win, obviously?
I do. I want Makosi to win as well, though, which is weird because I did hate her. She's been the way you should be on Big Brother. I'm dying to watch her. I take my hat off to the girl.

At the end of the day – come on, cut me some slack here: I had to! – Big Brother 6 finished on a uniquely moral, philosophical note. Here was the subliminal question it posed. Which do you choose: money or popularity? And here was the man who answered it, dollar signs lighting up behind the tears in his eyes. Eugene.

Eugene awoke on Thursday morning, day 77, a richer man monetarily, but clearly in a state of some advanced worry that he had croaked his spiritual wellbeing the night before. For it seemed to dawn on him that in taking the money he had not, as he had protested to Big Brother in the diary room, engineered a situation where there were two winners, pocketing their share of the winnings each. He had guaranteed that there was only one winner and that would be his accidental rival, Anthony. Who was going to reward the boy who had been so quick to reward himself, denying the public their right to choose in which pocket the allotted prize fund fitted? He struggled to maintain a chirpy face throughout the Garden Party mini task, knowing he had sold himself short. He kept on reiterating that he had made the wrong decision, and evidently what he meant was the wrong *moral* one.

Kinga made no bones about what she would have done in the situation, but then Kinga wasn't one for a moral conundrum. She spoke as she found. And she would have taken the money and run. But she would have taken the money with a smile on her face. When Kinga was eventually evicted, Davina hit the nail right on the head by declaring her a girl with a glorious lack of vanity. She couldn't have been righter. Very little with Kinga was cosmetic.

Anthony and Makosi both said they would have left the money for the winner, but then both Anthony and Makosi thought they were going to win Big Brother 6, somewhat muddying their pitch. It all begged the question, what do you go on Big Brother for? And in the end the answer is popularity. And Eugene ensured that Anthony was the most popular housemate. Ever since his date with Big Brother, the cheerful Geordie lad had emerged looking triumphant amid the collection of extravagant characters the production staff had put together this year. It struck me when I was interviewing Kemal that there were probably five, possibly more winners in the show this time and that the game had upped its own ante bounteously. At many points in the show Science, Derek, Kemal himself, Makosi for sure, Maxwell and even Saskia had looked as if they could whip the title of winner. But in the end it was little Anthony Hutton who had managed to stay amiable throughout his time in a house that would try the patience and virtue of a saint. He would give Big Brother an affable winner, in the

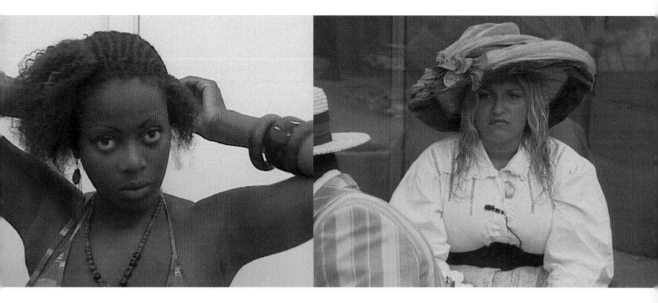

Which do you choose: money or popularity?

tradition of Craig from series 1 and Kate from series 3, rather than a starry one, in the manner of Brian from series 2 and Nadia from series 5. Eugene's moral hiccup meant that we were denied a second virgin winner, in the manner of Cameron, from series 4. What Anthony Hutton shared with all previous winners, and what was fast becoming a staple among Big Brother victors, was that eventually the good guy would always win out. Taking the money meant Eugene, who had hinted at that title ever since his arrival, fell at the last hurdle.

Day 78. Winners' day. The house rose in a peculiar mood, knowing that everything they had worked towards was coming to a close. Makosi tidied up her last ongoing narrative strand and settled the issue of her weave once and for all. She had asked Big Brother for a new afro, but his coiffure skills turned out to be lacking, perhaps explaining why he has such a propensity to stuff his house full of hairdressers

year after year. He denied her this one last request. But Makosi being Makosi, and knowing how to fashion a silk purse from any old sow's ear, she opted for a slicked-back number for the final night that looked frankly, well, fabulous.

Kinga was the first to be chucked to the lions. It came as no surprise to anyone, least of all Kinga herself, and the girl left with more affection hurled towards her than that wine bottle incident might have left any reasonable character to assume was her due. She was a good girl, too, but who could really have come in the house with 12 days to go, after one brief stint in the secret garden, and expect to do any better? She'd proved herself over and over by beating Craig in the popularity stakes. And she was a genius in her press conference, forgiving the other housemates for all that they'd punished her with and trying to forgive herself for the act that she knew her mother would blanch at.

If the world wasn't quite ready for Kinga, then Makosi just presented a raft of glorious contradictions that left her positively swimming in mystique. Without a shadow of a doubt, she was Big Brother 6's enigma, if not the whole brand's new most curious and beautiful face. If she had settled her weave storyline herself, it

was left to Craig to sort out once and for all the rather more serious matter of her whole pregnancy debacle – which by now it was clear had cost Makosi her public popularity – saying unequivocally to Davina when he was ejected that she was making up the story to create intrigue for a potential magazine buy-up. He said, and was later backed up by a rather furious-looking Anthony, that they had categorically not had sex, though he put it in rather fruitier language than that. Makosi struggled to establish the facts of her digital intercourse and subsequently freakish pregnancy scare to a braying press conference, though the sheer candour of her language stopped even the most hardcore tabloid hacks in their tracks: there was a lot of talk of wet genitals at the root of the confusion, if we want to get crude about this stuff. If Makosi was ultimately going to be remembered for being unfamiliar with the truth, it would be to diminish her considerable contribution to the house. As a series editor said while watching the VT of her best bits on eviction night, 'There wasn't a single storyline in that house that the girl wasn't directly involved in.' Though third, and booed, all the press wanted to talk to her.

The two boys left sitting on the orange sofas contemplating their fate, as Davina boomed her welcome into the house, made an odd, if not

unpleasant coupling. Anthony, bonding over grooming rituals like only he knew how, had given Eugene a spray tan earlier in the day, and they were both now rocking that distinct, Cat Deeley shade of burnt umber. It lent them a uniform, of sorts, though Anthony was as ever trussed up in Westwood and had scrunched his hair, while Eugene had opted for a checked shirt that was a little more High Street, not to say conservative. He knew what was coming, though Anthony had learnt to expect surprises on eviction nights, having seen both Kemal and Maxwell have their fates sealed against opponents he considered to be weaker. Davina called the result in.

'AND THE WINNER OF BIG BROTHER 6 IS …'

The pause lasted several lifetimes, maximizing the effect …

'ANTHONY!'

The lad did a bunny-hop circuit of the room, a bit of by now obligatory seventies dancing, and uttered his calling card 'Ding Dong' before saying the immortal line, 'Granny Hutton, I've done it … Alreet!'

Anthony and Eugene acquitted themselves manfully in both Davina's chat and the press conferences afterwards. Anthony even managed

'Ding Dong'

a couple of little funnies to cement his new-found notoriety. A girl from *More* magazine asked him if he'd like to be a TV presenter now, and he said that as he wasn't overly good at reading – 'It's not one of me strongpoints' – it didn't seem likely. His self-awareness was sweetly delivered.

Which is what we all wanted, really. Anthony looked at Eugene and put down the full stop that had marked the entire series, and a more fitting way you could not find to finish this particular Big Brother …

'END OF!' he said. We'll leave it there, shall we?

Profile:

KINGA
Karolczak

AGE: 20
STAR SIGN: Aries
HOME: London
JOB: Market Research

FIRST IMPRESSIONS: What an absolute hoot this one's going to be. Tiny, busty, brash. Loving the way she's wearing her weight, just bouldering through in the fig leaves and pushing her boobs up. Think there's a new Lesley coming into the house. She's got fun written all over her.

Kinga is 20 and the daughter of a Kuwaiti father and Polish mother. Prior to entering the secret garden, she was working as a market researcher at call centres in North Acton and Old Street, London, and living with her mum and stepdad. She has never lived away from home before and one of her motivations for going on Big Brother was to see what it would be like. Her other motivation was fame, of course. 'I don't deny it. I wanted to be noticed.' Kinga has a history with reality TV shows and was keen to get involved with *X-Factor* because of her singing voice. She had filled in an application form and done an audition for the show but decided against it when she started doing so well at the Big Brother auditions. 'The thing with Big Brother is that people get to know you as a person. And that it's the best one of the reality shows. Everyone knows that.' She has sung professionally before and she has a manager, Andy. Kinga has got an incredibly vivacious nature. 'I don't get pessimistic about anything. I always look for the good things. I have a motto: appreciate the things you've got and don't worry about the things you haven't. You can drive yourself mad wishing that you had more than you have, but some people have nothing. Be happy with what life has dealt you.' Her heroine is Jennifer Lopez, whom she met once after waiting five hours in the rain. 'She said two words to me. "Don't cry." And I immediately burst into tears.'

I meet Kinga at her hotel in St Albans the afternoon after the Big Brother final. She sweeps out of the car with a Louis Vuitton bag and a mobile pressed up against her ear and looks every inch the modern celebrity – though there are not many inches of her, bless her (she's 5 foot). Kinga has her mum and stepdad with her, both of whom are obviously as proud as anything of their little girl. Her similarity to a young Barbara Windsor is instantly astonishing. I mention this to her and she says, 'Yeah, there is something a bit *Carry On* about me, isn't there?' She's got bubbliness by the shed-load. I thought she was lovely.

How are you doing?
I feel really, really good. What I really enjoyed about last night was the press conference. I seemed to get a really good reaction from everyone there.

Tell me about your brief time in the house.
I got the call to go back into the house on the morning that Orlaith left. When she went, they called me and said somebody's outside waiting to pick you up, gather your stuff, you've got fifteen minutes to get it together, and before I knew it I was in the diary room getting ready to go back into the house. I didn't really have a chance to think about it even.

Had you counted out the idea of going back into the house?
Yeah, I didn't think it was going to happen, though I'd been watching it again by then and Orlaith did look really frail, as if she couldn't quite take what was going on in there. It's funny because Makosi put her in there because she said I was too young and couldn't cope with it, and actually it was Orlaith who couldn't cope with it.

Had you enjoyed being with Orlaith and Eugene in the secret garden?
I loved it in there but it drives you totally insane. If you want to know what it felt like, try locking yourself in a green room for three days with a cooker and two of your mates. Actually, make it two of your enemies. That'd be closer.

You didn't get on with them?
I liked Eugene and Orlaith to start with but she wore off after five minutes. I thought she was rubbish. She just slept and put moisturizer on. That's honestly all she did. She's the most boring person I've ever met in my life. She's all me, me, me. I didn't think she was beautiful but I did think she had a lovely figure. I don't get jealous about things like that, though. It's not as if she's Jennifer

Lopez or anything. I made a decision not to complain at all after watching her in the house. I don't think viewers want to see that. I thought she was ungrateful at the end of the day, but people see it differently.

Was it an advantage knowing about the housemates before you went in?
No. I was really looking forward to meeting them, though. I was dying to meet Craig, I basically love gay men. They are so much more fun than the straight ones. I was a little bit worried about the arguments because I'm more fun-loving than argumentative.

What did you want out of Big Brother?
I wanted to see what it was like living with other young people. I'm an only child and my mum does everything for me. I wanted to see if I could cope on my own in a different environment. I don't think I did too badly. It was quite an extraordinary experience for me.

It was a lovely thing that Davina said to you about having no vanity.
Yes, it was. Look, I know I'm not perfect and I don't pretend to be. If the papers want to call me a minger, then bring it on.

What did your mum say about the bottle incident? Was there an 'oh, Kinga!' moment?
My mum's very proud of me as you can see here. It's not nice for a mum to read in the papers everything that's been said about me but my mum's proud of whatever I do in life. Whatever I chose to do, so long as I was happy my mum would support me. And my stepdad's fantastic as well. They both are.

Do you personally regret the bottle incident?
I've got a bit of a sick sense of humour. I was drinking that night. And I thought it might be quite fun to take the mick. I wanted to take the mick. I know that it might obviously have offended a lot of people and I shouldn't have taken it that far but apparently they've written about me and about what went on all over the world so obviously I've created a bit of an impact. Big Brother is about doing things that haven't been done before. No one else can do that again on the show now. All you can do is laugh about it. You can't turn back time. Whatever you've done then you've done it for yourself and I don't have many regrets. Maybe I have a little regret about doing that but at the end of the day I know what happened. Craig can't say what happened because although both he and Makosi were fantastic characters in the house – probably the best – they were resentful of me coming in at the end and they didn't want me there. I didn't totally feel myself around them, so to speak! I'm in an amazing position here. Loads of people would love to be sitting here even if they'd done a poo in the middle of the garden. Think about how many people went through the auditions and didn't get in. I think I'm a very lucky girl.

Profile:
MAKOSI
Musambasi

AGE: 24
STAR SIGN: Libra
HOME: High Wycombe
JOB: Cardiac Nurse

FIRST IMPRESSIONS: Wow! Well, obviously she's gorgeous, but she radiates style and confidence, too. Has an Angie Stone look about her, if Angie Stone were a supermodel and ten stone lighter. Loving the afro. And loving a girl who understands jewellery. She's a real splash – looks like she's stepped off the cover of a magazine. Very into her.

Makosi is 24 and was born and raised in Harare, Zimbabwe. 'I had a beautiful childhood. My parents sacrificed a lot for me.' One of two daughters of a police officer father and housewife mother, she left the country at 18 to come to the UK to live with her aunt and to train as a nurse. She was following a family tradition: her grandmother was a village midwife in Zimbabwe. 'It was very cold when I got here, but I liked it.' Her other favourite celebrity nurse is Abi Titmuss. 'I think she's amazing and beautiful. I don't know why girls enjoy slagging her off.' Prior to entering the house she was working at the High Wycombe hospital in the commuter belt round London and living with her sister. She says she thinks it is unlikely that she will go back to nursing, but, as she tried to explain to Davina, she thinks of nursing as a state of mind and says that she genuinely wants to help people. Makosi attributes her astonishing self-confidence to her father. 'It all comes from him. My dad used to command people around as a senior police officer and I'd see him and think, hmm, I want to be like Daddy. I want to be able to keep such peace and order between people. To do that you need confidence and, honestly, I think it's charisma.' Makosi says that she has never been truly in love before. 'I've had people want to go out with me for my looks and use me as a kind of trophy. I've always guarded and protected myself from the "love" word.' Makosi says that her hero is Whitney Houston.

I meet Makosi at a photographer's studio on the day after the Big Brother final. Such has been her incredibly busy day that we have to snatch some time as she is having her hair and make-up done for a shoot with *Now* magazine. She has just finished what will turn out to be tomorrow's cover exclusive with the *News of the World*, an interview that the journalist, Rachel Richardson, is absolutely delighted with. Makosi has incredible strength and looks not at all perturbed by her rather harsh treatment on exiting the house. She is absolutely otherworldly. Whatever it is that constitutes star quality she has it by the bucket-load. But still the question remains as to whether the British public is ready for someone quite as radically prepossessing as she is. I was wowed by her, at any rate.

How do you feel that you did in the house?
Amazing. There are more ways of winning than being the last person to walk out of the house. I feel like I did tremendously.

Is all this attention vindication of how much interest you've generated in the house?
Yes. I had a meeting with a marvellous manager and agent this morning and signed up with him and it's rolling in. I do the *Sun* tomorrow and they've promised my agent they'll take back all the nasty things they've been saying about me. It's all talk, anyway. In the *Daily Mirror* today I had a whole page and Anthony had a quarter page.

Were you aware that the pregnancy story was going to hurt your house popularity quite as much as it did?
No way.

What about Craig's reasoning that you were perpetrating the tale to get a magazine deal?
I think Craig is a confused little boy. He's hardly the most reliable source when it comes to Anthony. He would have done anything to get that boy's attention. Did you see him whenever Eugene spoke to Anthony? It was horrifying. But I liked him. He was confused.

Honestly, do you think you trumped Kemal?
I think that Kemal was very threatened by me. He couldn't understand how somebody as normal as me could cause controversy and drama around themselves without having to resort to props. I don't mean it in a mean way, but he needed those stilettos for his story. He wanted to play the diva. Yes, he was threatened.

How was it seeing him last night?
Fabulous. The outfit was 'oh my gosh'. It was supposed to say this is not Makosi's night or Kinga's night or

Eugene's night or even the winner's night. It was supposed to say, this is Kemal's night. But he chose a wig similar to the one I'd been wearing for the last few days. If he'd known about the straight hair he would've come with a ponytail.

How do you feel about the booing?
I don't feel any worse. I feel like Davina had the power to make them cheer or boo for me and she decided for some reason to make them boo. That was for reasons that are up to her. I don't want to know why. It seemed like she wanted me to apologize for some reason and was set on getting that apology. I don't apologize because somebody I have never met before wants me to apologize. I apologize if I mean it and it comes from the heart.

How do you feel about the pool orgy now? Have you spoken to your family?
Yes. And they are loving it. My mum said, 'Look, you're 24. The way the press went on, it's like you're 12.' My sister, my mum and my dad are all behind me. Which feels nice.

You had a habit of taking the weaker girls under your arm in the house: Sam, then Vanessa. I tried to build people's characters. I genuinely wanted to see Eugene grow, which is why I chose him over Kinga. There was a journey to be had.

You were mortified that the producers put Kinga back in, right?
Right. At the end of the day, they can't make me evict her and then put her back in because of the emotional torment that causes both of us. I had rejected the girl once and then I had to face her again. I found it so difficult. How could she not be judging me? And how could we not resent her coming in at such a late stage in the game?

How do you feel about Anthony winning?
In his head Anthony thinks he's top dog. He was good looking but I couldn't have conversations with him. I am surprised I didn't win the show. Anthony was the politically correct person to win, if you like. Makosi lied, probably, that is what people would want to think, about having sex in the pool. So no, we don't want the liar to win. Anthony is an amazing guy but people have misunderstood me.

What about the accusation that you are an actress?
I've never acted before but I'd love to be an actress. I would love to be in Hollywood. But I wasn't acting in the house. If I was going to be an actress Halle Berry would have to watch her step.

What's your defining characteristic, Makosi?
Charisma.

Profile: EUGENE
Sully

AGE: 27
STAR SIGN: Sagittarius
HOME: Crawley
JOB: Engineer

FIRST IMPRESSIONS: He's goofy and really not at all comfortable in that fig leaf. Tears before bedtime, I'll be bound. Ticks the John Tickle box, and the Cameron thingy one. I don't think I really understand what that box represents but everyone seems to love it. Watch it – he'll probably win the blessed thing now.

Eugene is 27 and comes from Crawley in Sussex. Prior to entering the house he was working for the BBC, measuring radio transmitters. He had just finished a field trip on Radio Somerset when he got the Big Brother call and promptly handed in his notice. Eugene is not shy of becoming a spokesman for Radio technology. 'Engineering can be perceived as being quite dull, and what I've done is, while still making it seem quite geekish in a cool kind of way, sort of sexed up engineering. A lot of the people in that kind of industry can be quite introverted and intellectual. Part of the reason I'm probably not a brilliant engineer is because I'm not very serious and I'm quite flamboyant.' Eugene was living with his parents and his elder brother Gregory before entering the house. He says that his life splits into some quite distinct and separate parts. 'Because of my hobbies and interests there are my trendy friends who I go out to the cinema with or go out bowling with, but then I have my technical friends and we tend to have projects together: quad-biking, playing with engines, etc. Then there are my amateur-radio friends. I've had the ability with my different jobs to have different friends and play different roles for them.' Eugene says that his hero – 'or a person that I admire greatly' – is the writer and TV presenter Adam Hart-Davis. 'The thing I like about him is that he's so intelligent about his subject but incredibly enthusiastic, too.'

I meet Eugene in the garden of a hotel near Cockfosters in north London the morning after the Big Brother final. He is looking almost ridiculously bronzed after Anthony spray-tanned him in the house. He is practically fluorescent. It is drizzling but he is sitting under an umbrella eating a toasted sandwich. His brother Gregory is floating around and I have to drag him away from two ardent Eugene fans, an erudite couple from the States. Nerds are often thought to revert to technicalia out of some sort of social handicap, but Eugene is actually incredibly confident and, as we know, prone to rambling on with a story assuming you are as excited by it as he is, so he takes quite a bit of reigning in. But he oozes decency, for which basically he can be forgiven everything else. His excitability is engaging and infectious, but he is rather wearing company. If I'm being absolutely honest, I cannot imagine being stuck in the house with him without going a bit potty.

How are you feeling today, Eugene?
I'm in a very good mood. And getting some dinner down me helps. I was a little nervous earlier today. There are one or two offers being made and I got a slap on the wrist for ringing in to a couple of radio stations I used to work for.

Do you regret at all taking the money on Wednesday?
The problem is red mist. Red mist descends in certain situations, like driving, where you might drive closer to someone who is annoying you and yet you can't explain why you're doing it. In 60 seconds, with that kind of thought, my first reaction was to take the £50,000.

Did you feel it was a moral question, about the public being robbed of their right to choose a winner?
Yes, I did. I took half the prize money. I prefer the idea of winning the game, to be honest.

Do you think it cost you the game?
I think it might have cost me the game, yes. I seem to be quite popular since I've come out. But in the same sense, when I came out everyone seemed to cheer and really like me. What I have found out since is that most people would have taken the money option. Also I wasn't aware of the £200,000 offer, which was very clever on the part of Big Brother.

Are you a bit upset that that one moment of red mist might be seen as your defining contribution to the game?
Yes, a bit. But then everyone saw it as the right decision to make. Seeing it now I think it was. And it's neither here nor there whether I might've won £200,000. In the end what I do know is that I'm secure for the time being and that I might be able to improve my life in some way. I'm going to be sensible with it.

It wouldn't be a very Eugene thing to do to rush out and buy a Ferrari, would it?
No, I think if I was to buy a car I would probably buy something interesting, quirky and practical. That would be a bit more 'Eugene'. I'd like a Subaru SVX. It's got a long bonnet and lots of interesting features. They're quite weird.

Do you know what the producers liked about you in auditions?
I have a good idea of the type of person I am, yes.

You're actually very confident, aren't you?
Yes, I suppose so. It's improved over the last six weeks, that's for sure. Derek described me as being like a great British eccentric and that's the way that I'd like to see myself. It was a sweet description.

What were you expecting to get out of the Big Brother experience? Did you fancy the idea of being famous?
Oh, yeah. I mean I didn't, obviously, go into it thinking I would leave with a whole load of prize money and popularity. I sort of knew that wasn't going to happen. A number of people at the radio station I used to work at in Scotland used to tell me to go in for it and they said I'd be good on it. But I auditioned by accident. I had met a couple of the housemates from previous years – Cameron and Federico. They were really nice people. I didn't know what I expected out of it, if anything. I think I just went into it literally for the fun of it. I did not for one minute think I'd last until winners' week and get so very close to winning. I'm quite amazed that happened.

Was being liked a feature of it for you?
Yeah. I think what I wanted to do – because of my values, the things I believe in and the people that I associate with – I didn't want to make a fool of myself. I wanted to be myself.

You couldn't be anything but yourself, could you?
No. I think I was a sensible, subdued version of myself. One of the things you're asked before you go in is if you have a game plan and I said if I did it was only to be myself. The problem with playing any real game plan and trying to be someone that you're not or trying to get a relationship is then it's something that you have to keep bulletproof all the way to the end. Ultimately it's false.

Did Kinga see you through when Derek left?
Yes, she was very sweet. She is a sweet girl. I just don't like drunk people.

Derek 10 WEEK

Craig 11 WEEK

Kinga W

Makosi 11 WEEK

Eugene W